So You \
to Know About
THE
ENVIRONMENT

When **Bijal Vachharajani** is not reading Harry Potter, she can be found traipsing around the jungles of India or baking with chocolate. In her spare time, she works as a communications consultant and writes about education for sustainable development and food security, so she can fund those trips to the forest and buy those expensive Potter books. Bijal has a Master's in Environment Security and Peace with a specialisation in Climate Change and Security from the UN-mandated University for Peace in Costa Rica. Bijal was the editor of *Time Out*, Bengaluru, and has worked with *Sanctuary Asia* and 350.org. Her writing has appeared in *The Guardian*, *The Hindu*, *The Indian Express*, Scroll.in and Daily O, among other newspapers and magazines.

Sayan Mukherjee is an art supervisor in a leading advertising agency. He loves to dabble in paints, colours and is very passionate about his art. He carries his sketchbook wherever he goes. He lives in Kolkata.

So You Want
to Know About
THE
EnvironmenT

BIJAL
VACHHARAJANI

Illustrated by SAYAN MUKHERJEE

RED TURTLE

RUPA

For Reyansh.
Because you and your generation give me hope.

Published in Red Turtle by
Rupa Publications India Pvt. Ltd 2017
7/16, Ansari Road, Daryaganj
New Delhi 110002

Sales Centres:
Allahabad Bengaluru Chennai
Hyderabad Jaipur Kathmandu
Kolkata Mumbai

ISBN: 978-81-291-4512-3

First impression 2017

10 9 8 7 6 5 4 3 2 1

The moral right of the authors has been asserted.

Printed at Thomson Press India Ltd., Faridabad.

CONTENTS

Before you start reading this book, grab a pen or sharpen a pencil. You have to don your Sherlock Holmes deerstalker hat and exercise your little grey cells to make deductions as you read. You will need to investigate clues and scribble notes all over this book. And by writing in the margins, we end up saving paper and conserving trees, which makes us devious geniuses destined to save the world.
Insert maniacal laughter

CLIMATE CHANGE

RAIN, DEAR

Summer time was right around the corner. Winter had barely stuck around, the cold had vanished and the days had become hot, relentlessly hot. Ice creams melted faster than they could be eaten, classroom fans whirled slowly, and the bus journey home was unbearable with the smell of sweat and stale socks. Even the last-seat gang was exhausted from the heat and couldn't drum up the energy to bully anyone.

Since it was still early March, the teachers were huddled in their staff room, murmuring about climate change being responsible for this sudden heat wave. The Environment Studies teacher, Ms Shinibali, was looking rather smug. She was seen shaking her head and muttering, 'I warned everyone that this would happen' to anyone who would listen. Not many did.

Morning assembly had brought with it announcements like, 'Energy Saving' and 'Each student should do their bit to make their school proud'. Fans and lights were to be switched off before leaving the classroom, new energy-saving bulbs had replaced the flickering fluorescent tube lights at considerable cost, and class monitors were told to ensure that everyone did 'their bit'. It had become necessary—the papers said that there was going to be even more load shedding. That meant power cuts.

No air conditioning, no fans and no TV. How will we enjoy the summer vacation? And worse, how to charge all those gadgets with all those power cuts? Zeenat sighed and switched off her iPad. It was too hot to play *Temple Run*.

The blazing fire on the sides of the virtual maze was giving her a headache. Suddenly, her bedroom darkened. Zeenat looked outside her window, wondering what had happened.

Dark grey clouds hovered above her building. Zeenat gasped with delight as fat drops of rain began to slowly fall down—they plinked loudly on the window sill, landed with a soft whisper on the thirsty road, and glistened on the leaves of the peepal tree outside her window. The rain had come, bringing a smile to Zeenat's face.

She texted her friend Reyansh: 'It's raining. Goodbye heat!'

Two minutes later, Reyansh messaged back. 'SO NOT COOL! Rain in March! It's not the monsoon season. You do know that the rain can threaten our mangoes, right?'

Puzzled, Zeenat called up Reyansh. Mr-Know-It-All, as Reyansh was known in class, was also a Nerdfighter (yes, he is a John Green fan), and rattled off, 'Climate change, Zeenat, it's climate change.'

Zeenat rolled her eyes and said, 'I know, I know. It's causing this crazy heat and sudden rainfall. All of that stuff.'

'Exactly,' said Reyansh, warming up to his favourite topic. 'And this sudden rain could probably affect our mango crops. This early rain can damage it! That means, wait for it, fewer mangoes.'

A summer without mangoes? No mango milkshake, no slices of mango to suck on and no aam ras? Zeenat did not know how to even imagine that. The sudden rain was not very exciting suddenly.

What do you think: Is Zeenat's story a *Tall Tale* or *A Possible Real Deal*?

What Zeenat and Reyansh are talking about is **A Possible Real Deal**. Five points to Team Greenfidor, er... Team Green.

Zeenat and Reyansh's city, like many others across the globe, is currently facing unpredictable weather. This can have horrible implications not only for them, but also their neighbours and for people who live far away. It could create problems for habitats and animals. And the worst thing imaginable—the weather can also impact mangoes and chocolates (more on that later).

To understand this strange phenomenon that is gripping our planet, let's check out some facts and data.

SO TO BEGIN WITH, SOME SCIENCE

You should have studied this in Geography by now; if not, then go pester your teacher and ask—What is Climate and what is Weather? Or well, look it up on the Internet.

Got the answer? Made no sense? Got detention for asking questions? Okay, no, you didn't? Maybe because your teacher is not Miss Trunchbull (if you don't know who she is, go read *Matilda* by the wonderful Roald Dahl. No one is too old for that book. There's even a movie, if you're feeling too lazy). Maybe you got an answer, but didn't understand it.

No worries, let's make it simple.

Weather is the state of atmosphere which stays for a short period of time and is always changing. For example, to describe today's weather, what would you say? Today is ___.

Sunny

Dry

Cold

Rainy and Humid

Stormy

RACK YOUR BRAINS
Some days are very hot, and on some days it doesn't stop raining. Weather keeps changing—within hours or within weeks. Many phones now come with an in-built weather app which forecasts the day-to-day weather. What's the weather like today?

Climate is the average weather condition that prevails in an area over a long period of time (usually at least thirty years). It covers all sorts of conditions:

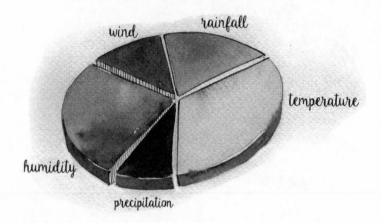

These conditions help scientists deduce what the climate of a particular area is. And different parts of the world have different climates. The climate of a place can change over a long time; we're talking millions of years. But weather can change much faster, on a moment-to-moment, day-to-day, season-to-season, and year-to-year basis.

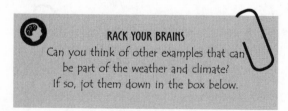

RACK YOUR BRAINS
Can you think of other examples that can be part of the weather and climate? If so, jot them down in the box below.

_____

_____

_____

_____

_____

_____

_____

_____

_____

If you have been paying attention in Geography, you would know that there are five main climate groups. They are:

Tropical: Moist and Monsoon
Dry: Arid and Semi-Arid
Mild: Mediterranean, Humid subtropical, and Marine
Continental: Warm Summer, Cool Summer, and Subarctic
Polar: Tundra and the ice caps

What is India's climate like? Circle the answer from the choices above. (Answer: _Tropical wet and dry. Also semi-arid in certain areas_)

RACK YOUR BRAINS
If you have travelled to different Indian cities or even countries, write down the names of five places and then draw the climates that you have experienced.

The climate is changing—weather you like it or not!

According to the Intergovernmental Panel on Climate Change[1] (a scientific, intergovernmental body that comes under the United Nations, also known as the IPCC), the term climate change 'refers to a change in the state of the climate that can be identified (e.g. using statistical tests) by changes in the mean and/or the variability of its properties, and that persists for an extended period, typically decades or longer.

It refers to any change in climate over time, whether due to natural variability or as a result of human activity.' (That's right. The climate can change on its own, and also people can change it.)

'In the United Nations Framework Convention on Climate Change (UNFCCC), climate change refers to a change of climate that is attributed directly or indirectly to human activity that alters the composition of the global atmosphere and that is in addition to natural climate variability observed over comparable time periods.'[2]

WHAT ARE THEY TALKING ABOUT? SPEAK ENGLISH, SOMEONE. ANYONE?

Simply put—the climate is changing. And pretty fast.

As sun rays enter the Earth's atmosphere, most of the heat is released back by our planet. But some of that heat

---

[1] www.ipcc.ch/publications and data/ar4/syr/en/mains1.html

[2] https://unfccc.int/files/essential_background/background_publications_htmlpdf/application/pdf/conveng.pdf

stays back, trapped by the Green House Gases (or GHGs, like carbon dioxide) in the atmosphere. That is actually a good thing because GHGs are needed to sustain life as we know it on Earth. Think of the GHGs as a huge mosquito net stretched over our atmosphere, and instead of keeping out the mosquitoes, they are trapping heat which we all need. Pity they don't trap mosquitoes instead.

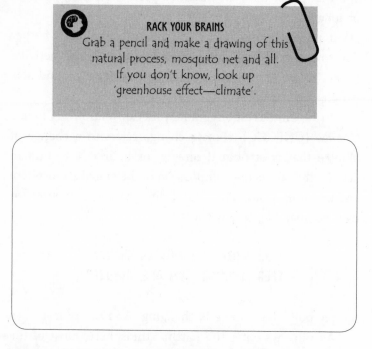

RACK YOUR BRAINS
Grab a pencil and make a drawing of this
natural process, mosquito net and all.
If you don't know, look up
'greenhouse effect—climate'.

Now, there's a bit of a problem in this process.

Humans have been pumping too many GHGs into the atmosphere by burning coal, cutting down trees, flying too many planes and driving too many cars. As more and more

GHGs are trapped in the atmosphere, the planet is getting hotter, and that's causing **global warming**.

The main culprits (who are also the good guys in moderation) are:

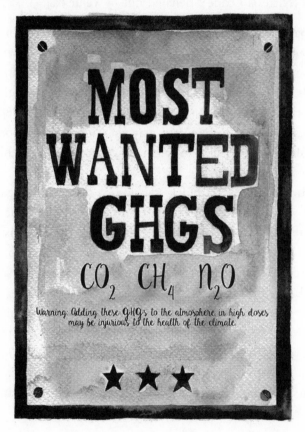

MOST WANTED GHGS

CO_2 CH_4 N_2O

Warning: Adding these GHGs to the atmosphere in high doses may be injurious to the health of the climate.

★ ★ ★

CO_2 (Carbon Dioxide): Released when we burn fossil fuels such as coal, oil and gas and when we clear land by cutting trees and forests.

CH_4 (Methane): Burped and farted by farm animals, especially cows; emitted from wastelands and landfills. Also, methane is released during waste water treatment.

N_2O (Nitrous Oxide): Belched out by vehicles.

Global warming means that there is an increase in the average temperature in the air and the ocean, snow and ice are melting at an alarming rate and as a result, sea levels are rising. This average rise in temperature is a global occurrence, not necessarily in every specific location. Some places that used to be warm may get cooler or have longer winters. But overall, the Earth is warmer. And all this is part of **climate change.**

Imagine Jenga, a block-stacking-crashing offline game. One wrong move and the entire towering block that you had carefully constructed can tumble down. Nature is like Jenga—our water, our air, our land, and even all of us are connected to the climate. As you may have observed, usually the Earth knows how to regulate her own climate (she's quite smart. Oh yes, Earth is a woman). But the amount of GHGs we are deliriously pumping into the atmosphere is beyond the Earth's regulation capacity.

Just as the Jenga blocks fall fast, different earthlings—plants, animals—have a difficult time adapting to this rapidly changing environment.

The fuss over fossil fuels

The Industrial Revolution, which took place in the eighteenth and nineteenth century, was marked with rapid developments in industrial manufacturing across Europe and North America. Since then we have been heavily dependent on fossil fuels, whether it is for living, transportation or agricultural purposes.

Fossil fuels are called non-renewable sources of energy, because they're exactly that—if we keep pumping them out of the ground, they will run out at some point. Until then we will keep going further and further to look for them in deep seas or tar sands, which can be terrible for the environment, and expensive for us.

Also, there is increased pollution because we are using too many fossil fuels, which further contributes to climate change. That's why people are asking governments across the world to look at renewable forms of energy such as solar, wind, and water.

The magic number: 350

Climatologist James Hansen was one of the first scientists to make noise about climate change. Here's what he said:

'If humanity wishes to preserve a planet similar to that on which civilization developed and to which life on Earth is adapted, paleoclimate evidence and ongoing climate change suggest that CO_2 will need to be reduced from [current levels] to at most 350 ppm.'[1]

350 parts per million (ppm) is the safe level of carbon dioxide molecules in the atmosphere.

We are already above 400 ppm! So basically, if we want a world similar to the one we have now, we must cut back.

---

[1]http://350.org/about/science/

Visit *www.co2.Earth* to check the atmospheric CO_2 levels of various cities.

Graph reproduced with permission from 350.org

There's even a group called 350.org—they are 'building a global grassroots climate movement that can hold our leaders accountable to the realities of science and the principles of justice.'[1]

In 2010, as part of their 350 Earth campaign, aerial artist Daniel Dancer and 3,000 children of Ryan International School, Rohini in Delhi came together to form an image of an elephant. They wanted to remind political leaders that climate change is the elephant in the room. (That phrase is used when people are ignoring something.) Look up *art.350org/EARTH*.

---

[1] http://350.org/how/

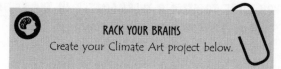

RACK YOUR BRAINS
Create your Climate Art project below.

IF YOU WERE TO STICK A THERMOMETER IN THE EARTH'S ARMPIT RIGHT NOW, WHAT WOULD IT SAY?

Thermometers don't speak. (Actually they do, as there are talking thermometers. So there.)

But back to the question—the thermometer would show that the Earth is getting warmer than ever before in the history of mankind. According to the National Oceanic and Atmospheric Administration's (NOAA's) National Climatic Data Center[1], in 2014, 'the global temperature was 1.24°F (0.69°C) above the long-term average for the 20th century'. They have data dating back to 1880! And from then, 2014 turned out to be the warmest year officially on record. After that 2015! And the mercury, it seems, just keeps on rising.

In December 2015, world leaders met in Paris where many of them agreed to limit the global average temperature increase to 1.5 to 2°C. Fingers crossed!

BUT LOTS OF PEOPLE SAY THAT CLIMATE CHANGE IS NOT REALLY HAPPENING. I MEAN… HUMANS CAN'T POSSIBLY CHANGE THE WEATHER, IT'S JUST A NATURAL PHENOMENON.

It's true that the climate is always changing and has been changing for some five billion years now. But over the last century, the problem is that human activity—such as fossil fuel burning, population burst, pollution, deforestation—is accelerating the change. We are sending up GHGs into the atmosphere when we burn fossil fuels. We're sending too

---

[1]https://www.ncdc.noaa.gov/sotc/global/201412

much, too fast for Earth to rebalance it on her own. This is called the Anthropocene age—where human beings are impacting the planet with their actions.

Of course, natural phenomena, such as when a volcano erupts, adds tons and tons of CO_2 into the atmosphere. Annually, the gross total CO_2 they emit is around 260 million metric tons! Yet, now humans are adding 30 billion metric tons of CO_2 to the atmosphere—that's 100 times more than the poor volcanoes.[1] Humans: 100. Volcanoes: 1.

Around 97 per cent of prominent climate scientists agree that climate change is a fact.[2] Here's what they say, 'Climate-warming trends over the past century are extremely likely due to human activities.'

P.S.: For the purpose of this book, we will ignore the wee 3 per cent and not concern ourselves with 'climate-change deniers'.

---

[1] www.skeptical science.com/volcanoes-an-global-warning.htm

[2] http://climate.nasa.gov/scientific-consensus/

I know for a fact that not all places on the planet are heating up. (Ha! Got you there.) Some parts are actually getting cooler—so much for global *warming*.

One more time—s...l...o...w...l...y this time—global warming is the gradual increase in Earth's temperature. With more amount of carbon in the atmosphere, the climate is changing and making the weather more unpredictable (kind of like the class teacher's mood when you haven't done your homework).

For example, when the Earth gets heated up, the oceans absorb some of the heat. Throw in some melting ice caps next. And what you see is that the oceans expand due to the heat and extra water from the melting ice caps. Pretty much like boiling a pot of water, and then adding more water to it. What do you think will happen? It will boil over.

As oceans become warmer, that means the major air currents get intensified, and we can expect stormier weather. There could be heavier rainfall or snowfall as well. As oceans expand, we can expect more floods.

At the same time, the warming of the planet can mean droughts in already water-starved areas because in some places it means lesser rainfall. And because the Arctic is getting hotter, Korean and European scientists[1] have found that it creates what they call 'a bulge of warm air in the lower atmosphere'. Now this forces the jet streams—which are fast moving air currents in the upper atmosphere—to

---

[1] https://insideclimatenews.org/news/31082015/yes-warming-arctic-means-cold-winters-elsewhere-Boston-US-Asia

dip further south in some place. The jet stream carries cold Arctic air causing extreme cold in some regions!

Remember, the increase in temperature is calculated on a global average, which means as a whole, the Earth is getting warmer. Specific locations may differ, and weather changes on a day-to-day basis, even if the longer trend of climate says something different.

Everything is connected—once something changes in one place, it will have repercussions in other parts of the system.

Meet the people who created smog meringues

Can you eat smog? Yes, according to Zack Denfeld, one of the founders of The Center for Genomic Gastronomy. In case you're wondering, smog is a type of pollution, usually a mix of smoke from coal and sulphur dioxide. UGH!

Fog + Smoke = Smog.

When you whip egg, what happens? Air gets trapped as the egg foams, right? If you have ever eaten a meringue, then you know it's basically egg whipped until it becomes stiff white peaks. Sugar is added and then it's baked. Meringues taste amazing with whipped cream and strawberries.

The people at the CGG realized that egg foams are up to 90 per cent air. So they trooped off to various places across the world, to beat smog into eggs to harvest air pollution!

They first conducted the experiment in Bengaluru, where they went to different locations and whipped the eggs along with dollops of polluted air. This was then baked and displayed on a map of the city. The batter can be tested to see how much pollutants it contains. Smog, said Zack, can be tasted and compared this way. You definitely don't want to eat these, but would be fun to whip up a smog egg meringue. What say?

Rewind July 2015

As the month of July slips into the calendar year, it's time to dust those umbrellas and raincoats. Teachers start to wonder how they will complete their term portion, while students rejoice at the thought of a rainy holiday. Tiger reserves close for the monsoon to allow the forest to replenish without the steady footfall of human beings, streams fill to the brim, and tigers make tiger cubs in peace (without tourists gawking at them). In villages, farmers sow seeds in anticipation of a healthy rainfall, which will nourish the seeds, nudging them to grow into fluffy cotton balls or shiny purple brinjals, or tall stalks of paddy that wave happily in the wind.

But 2015's July didn't bring with it the promise of rain for farmers in Telangana. Already, the year was threatening to be hotter than 2014, the warmest year on record since 1880[1]. A newly formed state, Telangana was witnessing one of its worst heat waves. Farmers waited for the rain, with the cotton and soya seeds sown, but there wasn't any rain to even plough their fields. By August, the region

---

[1]https://www.nasa.gov/press/2015/january/nasa-determines-2014-warmest-year-in-modern-record/

had a deficit rainfall of minus 21 per cent[1] (that's a lot, by the way).

What can such a scenario possibly mean?

a. Less rice, because Telangana farmers grow paddy and the crop needs a lot of water.

b. More problems for the farmers who are forced to borrow money from crooked moneylenders. These moneylenders charge crazy interest rates for loans—even up to 60 per cent.

c. Water problems for people.

Answer: All of the above!

---

[1] http://timesofindia.indiatimes.com/city/hyderabad/Bad-monsoon-killing-Telangana-farmers-crops-and-water-supply/articleshow/48367921.cms

Weirding, all of this

A lot of scientists and activists are using the phrase 'Global Weirding', which according to their website, explains 'how the rise in average global temperature leads to all sorts of crazy things—from hotter heat spells to colder cold spells, more drought and intense flooding, as well as slow-onset changes such as ocean acidification and sea level rise. Also includes oddball things such as jellyfish clogging up the pipes of nuclear power plants, forcing them to shut down.' You can check out *http://www.globalweirding.is/here* to see what different scenarios of temperature rise can mean for the planet and for us.

? Huh fact of the day

It's against the law to use the words 'climate change' in Florida and Wisconsin in the USA in certain departmental papers. In Florida, they are calling it 'Extreme Weather Events'.

RACK YOUR BRAINS

If you were living in Florida or Wisconsin, then how would you tell someone about climate change? Think of different words to describe the phenomena. Here are some word combinations (with the help of a thesaurus of course).

⬦ Metamorphosis of atmospheric conditions
⬦ An about-face of meteorological character

Don't they sound like Very Important Words? What words would you be able to invent?

_____

_____

_____

_____

_____

_____

_____

ARE WE ALL GOING TO BE TOAST? OR WELL, ROASTED LIKE KHAKHRAS?

The fact is that Earth will adapt to these changes; just as she has in the past. Humans, and some other earthlings, may not be so lucky. We are already facing many issues related to climate change and we don't even realize it.

▸ **Unpredictable weather:** Unpredictable weather can wreak havoc upon harvest that includes mangoes and cacao beans (the main ingredient in chocolate). In Africa, the weather is becoming too dry to grow cacao. And pests are also attacking the pods! That means farmers will grow lesser cocoa and grow other crops to make ends meet. And all this while, we have been eating too much chocolate, far more than the supply. The world is not going to be a good place without chocolate and good food, that we can agree upon.

▸ **Huge losses:** Unpredictable weather leads to a loss of human life and infrastructure. Some of the changes we've seen are extreme events like hurricanes, tsunamis, tornados, etc. that are occurring more often and more severely. Storms are bigger, faster, more frequent, and more unpredictable than they were before. For example, people could lose their houses or even their lives in a flood, like the one which hit Chennai in 2015. Or a tornado could crumble down a school building. No school for a while sounds fun, but forever? Nah!

▶ **Habitat loss:** It's not just us, even animals are suffering, thanks to umm... us. Species are getting threatened with extinction at a faster rate than ever. In 2016, Australian scientists declared the Bramble Cay melomys[1], a critically endangered mosaic-tailed rat to be extinct! And they think human-induced climate change is the culprit.

▶ **Costing us a pretty paisa:** All of this is creating a huge dent in our collective wallets, because governments have to figure out how to repair all these problems. In 2012, a study called, 'Climate Vulnerability Monitor: A Guide to the Cold Calculus of a Hot Planet'[2] found that climate change is 'contributing to the deaths of nearly 400,000 people a year and costing the world more than $1.2 trillion, wiping 1.6 per cent annually from global GDP'. (That's Gross Domestic Produce) This is just the beginning. Imagine the costs if things get worse.

▶ **Health issues:** We all know that the weather affects our

[1]https://www.theguardian.com/environment/2016/jun/14/first-case-emerges-of-mammal-species-wiped-out-by-human-induced-climate-change
[2]http://www.theguardian.com/environment/2012/sep/26/climate-change-damaging-global-economy

health. According to the World Health Organisation[1], 'climate change will also affect infectious disease occurrence'. Respiratory illnesses from air pollution may seem obvious, but there's a long list of diseases including malaria, dengue and cholera from water contamination.

? WHO knew

According to the World Health Organisation, as far back as the late 19th century, humans knew about the link between climatic conditions and epidemic diseases. Roman aristocrats would head off to the hills during the summer to avoid malaria, which sounds suspiciously like what the Britishers did in India.

▸ **Climate refugees:** As sea levels rise, islands are going to get engulfed by water, and people will be forced to leave their homes. It's already happening—a documentary film, *Sun Come Up*, tells the story of the Carteret Islanders, a community living in the South Pacific Ocean, who are forced to look for a new home because of rising sea levels. Earlier in 2016, news filtered in that five tiny islands that were part of the Solomon Islands in the Pacific went under water[2]! Luckily, no one lived there. But their neighbouring islands are seeing their villages destroyed by water. If you think 'It's not my problem', then imagine for a minute what it would feel like to

---

[1] http://www.who.int/globalchange/environment/en/chapter6.pdf
[2] https://www.theguardian.com/environment/2016/may/10/five-pacific-islands-lost-rising-seas-climate-change

lose your home because someone else was sending up carbon in the atmosphere! How awful would that be?

▶   **A cranky planet:** When it's hot, you become cranky; and if you're stuck in the rain with your school books being soaked inside a non-waterproof school bag, it is just not happy news. And now research shows that weather impacts our mood, and that means with unpredictable weather, our moods could also be pretty much unpredictable.

Climate change affects all of us in different ways—from plummeting and rising temperatures to unpredictable weather patterns, complicated health issues and it also threatens food security and livelihoods. Let's face it, the planet will adapt. We, the human species, may not be so lucky. Ignoring these problems may just show that our empathy levels are slowly eroding away, being washed away by rising sea levels and melting away in this ferocious heat. Uh oh.

Adapt and/or mitigate?

Countries across the world are looking to reduce climate change impacts in two ways:

▶   **Mitigation:** Reducing or removing the GHG emissions; which mean moving to cleaner energy sources to reduce the emissions. Or removing them by technological methods (see the postcard on geo-engineering to get a teensy-weensy idea).

‣ **Adaptation:** Looking at ways to reduce the impacts of climate change through systemic change to limit the damage. For instance, farmers could perhaps grow different kinds of crop in the same field, some of which are drought-resistant or start rainwater harvesting in preparation for delayed monsoon.

Postcard from Greg Branch
Geo-engineering: A temporary fix or a solution?

Greg Branch is the coolest stay-at-home dad who wrote an entire thesis (that's a tediously long research essay you have to write to get a Master's degree) on geo-engineering. He lives in Washington D.C. in the USA after living in Central America where he was affiliated with the U.S. Peace Corps.

Okay, so what if climate change starts creating such havoc that even reducing our carbon emissions wouldn't change a thing for decades? We don't want the climate to get to an emergency state of health. In case it does, people are talking about what a climate operating room might be able to do. Scientific doctors have come up with a possible emergency response to climate change. It's called geo-engineering: a way to engineer the planet so that humans can temporarily fix the problem we have gotten ourselves into.

There are two categories of geo-engineering.

Carbon Removal and Storage: Removing carbon from the atmosphere so the heat isn't trapped as much and then storing it somewhere safe sounds really hard, but scientists have identified the four best ways to do it. This includes putting scrubbers at the end of smokestacks to catch carbon as it's produced, removing carbon from the air by placing collectors on hillsides, planting more trees to suck up carbon through photosynthesis, or drowning it in the ocean!

Solar Reflection Management: This means reflecting the sun's heat away from the Earth so it doesn't heat up any longer. Scientists plan to do this by creating more clouds by spraying the ocean's water into the sky using ships, building giant space mirrors that create shadows on the Earth, and injecting sulphur into the stratosphere to cool the planet. There you have it. Just like our own health, we need to take care of ourselves to avoid a medical emergency. These are technological interventions which can get quite warped, and some of them sound drastic and dire. Maybe you will be the next to have an idea to cool the planet!

TO DO OR NOT TO DO, THAT'S REALLY UP TO YOU

ACTION 1
What's your climate quotient?

When it comes to carbon emissions, here's your chance to play Fastest Fingers First and show off how climate-savvy you are. Some activities in our daily lives are extremely carbon-intensive, which means they release more carbon into the atmosphere, while others are more environment-friendly and help save or 'sequester' carbon emissions.

To play this quiz, give yourself a T if you pick the first answer, a Y for the second one and a W for the third one.

1. When you travel to school
   a. The chauffeur drops you by car
   b. You carpool, bike or take the school bus
   c. You get there, depending on your mood that day
2. Your art teacher gives you a craft project
   a. You go out and buy a hobby kit and complete the assignment
   b. Think creatively and use recycled material for the project
   c. Your dog ate up the project note, so you couldn't complete it
3. Your room is beautifully lit up with
   a. Yellow and fluorescent bulbs and tube lights
   b. CFL and LED lights and lots of sunlight during the day
   c. You share your room with your annoying sibling so it's dark all the time
4. When on a family trip, you prefer to
   a. Buy bottles of water from the railway station or airport
   b. Carry reusable water bottles for each member
   c. Not drink water, because too much time is spent looking for toilets

5. When you open your lunchbox, it's usually
   a. A fruit like blueberry
   b. A Kinnaur apple
   c. You hate fruits

6. The folks are off shopping, they
   a. Go hands free and pay 10 rupees for plastic shopping bags
   b. Carry their own cloth bag
   c. Only shop online

7. It's your birthday, and you serve your birthday cake in
   a. Thermocol disposable plates and spoons
   b. Good old steel plates
   c. What cake? Most of it is on your face.

8. Your brother (or whoever's the masterchef in your house) made rajma and there were leftovers. You
   a. Chucked them in the bin
   b. Made a burrito the next day
   c. Cannot stand beans of any kind, who wants to fart all day

CALCULATE YOUR SCORE

Mostly Ts
Tsk Tsk! Terrible: Get cracking, you have lots of work to do before you can be part of Team Greenfidor.

Mostly Ys
YAYY! Go Team Greenfidor: You are a bona fide member of the green team. Now go on, spread the word.

Mostly Ws
Whatever: Yeah, whatever. You need to get your priorities straight and then come back and take the quiz again.

ACTION 2
Debate the science

Prep yourself for a debate, but as a climate change denier. Come up with arguments about how climate change is a natural process and humans are not accelerating it. Now, look for holes in your own arguments. Who won?

_____

_____

_____

_____

_____

_____

_____

_____

_____

_____

_____

_____

_____

_____

_____

_____

_____

_____

_____

_____

_____

_____

ACTION 3
Map your family's moods

You can do this on your tablet or in a notebook (the one with pages, not the laptop). As the weather changes, see if it affects you and your family's mood. Does your annoying sibling become more annoying when it's really hot outside? Or does your dad nag you a little bit more when it's raining unseasonably and he's behaving unreasonably as well?

Use emoticons to illustrate their mood. Keep this up for a month, and then share the results with the family.

The Family	Sunny day	Rainy day	Pleasant day	Meh day	Hot day
Sibling	⌣	⌣	⌣	⌣	⌣
Mum		⌣			
Dad					
Grandparent					
Me!					

ACTION 4
Calculate your carbon footprint

A carbon footprint is the total amount of GHG emissions generated by a person, a product, or a group. This book isn't going to give you lengthy calculations here. Hit the Internet to calculate if you're treading or trampling upon the Earth's atmosphere.

Visit: *http://no2co2.in/CarbonCalculator.php*

Swap results with your friends, teachers, and family. Now think of ways you can individually and as a group, bring down your carbon emissions. And if you do stumble upon a solution, then let us in as well.

By the way:

- In 2005, the average per capita footprint of an Indian was 1.6 tons of CO_2 emissions per year.
- Globally, the average is 3.9 tons. Developed countries, historically, are responsible for 79 per cent of emissions from 1850 to 2011. And that's why a lot of developing countries are demanding that the developed countries take on the climate responsibility. That is called, 'common but differentiated responsibility'.

That means on an average, Indians are emitting less carbon, but with rapid, unplanned development that could change drastically. Plus, we have a massive population. Even if we are doing better than some countries, we can still improve!

ACTION 5
Air test drive

How do you test air quality, if you don't have fancy kits[1] like scientists do? Here's a simple experiment that you can do at home.

You will need a wire hanger (ask your folks before taking one from the cupboard) and some thick, strong rubber bands.

Bend open the hanger to make it wider. Now stretch two rubber bands on each side of the hanger. Hang the hanger outside the window, in a balcony, wherever you want to test for pollutants. As the days go by, the more brittle—cracked and hard—the rubber bands become, the more pollutants in the air.

Try the same experiment in a park, near an industrial area and see if the results are different. Psst: NEVER EVER go to strange places alone—always take an adult you trust with you.

---

[1] http://lifestyle.howstuffworks.com/crafts/other-arts-crafts/science-projects-for-kids-weather-and-seasons7.htm

FOOD

THE MYTH OF 'AN APPLE A DAY KEEPS THE DOCTOR AWAY'

Hashim hated apples. His dad kept buying them, along with bananas. He preferred grapes and strawberries and even a banana sometimes, thank you very much. But they weren't available all through the year, unlike the dreaded apples.

His father would cluck at him and say, 'An apple a day keeps the doctor away' and make him eat up all the apple slices. One day, while reading the book *The Tastemaker: Why We're Crazy for Cupcakes But Fed Up With Fondue*, Hashim had a eureka moment.

So next day at breakfast, Hashim put on his best I-Know-It-All voice and informed his entire family that their dad's favourite phrase didn't come from a doctor. It was actually coined by a man called J.T. Stinson, an apple horticulturist from Missouri. According to the book, in 1904, Stinson used that line to promote apples at a world fair, and since then everyone thinks apple = healthy. 'How about that?' said Hashim. 'A marketing line has somehow become a health mantra for at least a century now.'

Hashim's dad, who had turned a shade of red rather like a Gala apple, recovered quickly. 'You do know right, that doesn't mean apples are not healthy for you. An apple packs in fibre and Vitamin C. You need a healthy diet to keep the doctor away and that can include apples since they are good for you. So, Hashim, finish your apple.'

Ah, parents shall never be told that they are wrong.

Variety is the spice of life

Our food system is complex and diverse, and that's what makes it fun and interesting. Life would be dull as dudhi if you have to eat a gourd every day. Let's take a look at the different kinds of fruits and vegetables that you can try.

A for Apple, lots of apples

In the Jurassic Age, when your parents and grandparents were children, they used to have something like *two* choices of apples! One was a crisp red apple and the other a golden apple that was tart and juicy. Both apples came from the hilly regions of the north—Kashmir and Himachal Pradesh.

Today, take a walk down the supermarket aisle that stocks apples. At last count, we were importing waxy red Washington apples, pale reddish yellow Fuji ones (though these are now grown in India as well), candy Green apples, and crimson Red Prince, and Gala and Chilean apples. Closer home there's Red Delicious from Himachal Pradesh, Royal Delicious grown widely in India, Golden Delicious from Jammu and Kashmir, and Himachal Pradesh, and McIntosh from Uttar Pradesh and Himachal Pradesh. And that's only naming a few apples! There are more than 7,500 varieties of apples in the world. If your parents once thought there were just two kinds of apples, now they know better.

Of course, variety is good. But that's the local variety. Too much variety of food that travels from different parts of the world to your market can be bad for the environment (more on that later).

❓Did you know?
There's an apple called the Winter Banana Apple because it has a banana-like flavour.

B is for Brinjal, lots of brinjals

Brinjal is the easiest vegetable to spot.

▶ There's the big fat purple aubergine that looks like an obese but squat baseball bat. That's perfect for roasting on the flame and making a baingan bharta or baba ghanoush.

▶ The small eggplant, that's shaped like an egg, makes a yum vegetable or stir fry. It comes in purple and green colours. And also in white!

▶ The long and light green brinjal is used extensively in Maharashtrian cooking.

So many kinds of brinjals and so many names for them! That's called biodiversity.

C is for Come on, you can take it from here

Even though there is so much variety in food, we keep eating the same kind, like eating only basmati rice or just wheat at home. The Food and Agriculture Organisation estimates that since the 'beginning of this century, about 75 per cent of the genetic diversity of agricultural crops has been lost.'[1]

Despite this, there're still plenty of options being grown in the fields! Like different kind of flours made out of finger millet (ragi), pearl millet (bajra), and sorghum (jowar). They all have different textures and tastes, adding a lot more flavour to food.

But because there's market demand for one kind of rice or wheat, it becomes easily available and cheaper. And we get lesser biodiversity on our plates! Isn't it boring to eat just one kind of food day in, and day out? Now that should give us some Fear Of Missing Out on cool food.

RACK YOUR BRAINS
Make a list of all the different varieties of fruits and vegetables you have ever eaten. For instance, there's green lady's finger, but you also get red okra (same veggie, different name)! Then there're different kinds of cabbage—white and green, as well as a crunchy purple one.

---

[1]http://www.fao.org/docrep/007/y5609e/y5609e02.htm

Climate-smart foods

Millets are called climate-smart grains because they can grow even in drought-like conditions as they don't need much water. They can also grow in high temperature and poor soil.

A DINNERTIME THREAT

If we were to get a rupee for every time we were told to eat up our food because children in Africa are starving, by now, we would be richer than Bill Gates. Okay, almost richer.

Actually, what they don't tell you is that with 204 million undernourished people, India is leading in the world hunger list. India has more undernourished people[1] than all of sub-Saharan Africa.

Why is that? Isn't there enough food for everyone in the world?

There is enough food to go around across the globe. In fact, according to Oxfam, we are producing at least seventeen per cent more food per person than we did thirty years ago[2]. Yet there are people who don't have enough food to eat. At least a billion of them! Let's take a look at some of the reasons:

---

[1] http://www.fao.org/focus/e/sofi/Count-e.htm

[2] http://www.oxfam.ca/there-enough-food-feed-world

▸ Smallholder farmers (who own small pieces of land) are often forced to sell all their produce in the market at a loss, and don't have enough to eat. And they grow the food we eat!

▸ There are people who don't have enough money to buy food, or don't have access to nutritious food. Many can't afford to buy good quality, nutritious food.

▸ In some countries, buying junk food is cheaper than buying fruits and vegetables! Yes, the prospect of eating burgers and fries is exciting for a few days. It's not really the healthiest option. And if that's all you can afford to eat, then it loses its appeal quickly.

LETTUCE TAKE A CLOSER LOOK AT OUR FOOD SYSTEM

How did we start growing all of this stuff? For that, let's step back in the past.

Human beings used to be hunter-gatherers. Small groups hunted for animals in the wild. They also gathered edible roots, nuts, berries (can you imagine, the kind of trial and error that had happened here? *Grunt*... do you think that mushroom's tasting a bit off, Oops! Thunk!)

But then, some 13,000 years ago, people began sowing seeds and growing crops. Animals were domesticated for meat, milk, and their skin.

Then came the Industrial Revolution in the eighteenth and nineteenth centuries, and machines began to crop up in farms.

By the twentieth century, there were bigger machines to grow tonnes of food. Pesticides and fertilizers popped up around this time. As more food was grown, soil nutrition was being depleted at a faster rate, and synthetic chemicals were used to enrich the soil.

And as farms became more mechanized, animals also began to be 'grown' in a manner that would be more economic and boost productivity. Cows, hens, pigs and goats were crammed into spaces called factory farms, with barely any space to move about. Food and water was provided to them, along with antibiotics and growth hormones.

In the late twentieth century, genetic alterations were made to seeds so that plants can survive drought or fight against a particular pest. These are called Genetically Modified seeds.

And now? In the twenty-first century, we are growing more food but not feeding our entire planet. We are forcing animals into battery cages, dingy sheds and crowded, unlit barns. Indiscriminate use of pesticides and chemical fertilizers is harming the soil, making it less fertile and, thus, reducing yields. Food is processed until it's almost unrecognisable; or, frozen or treated with processes so that it can be eaten even when it's not being grown seasonally. Food is not always eaten in the same place it is grown in—this adds to the carbon emissions and increases food prices along the way because of transport.

OKAY, SO WE ARE GROWING FOOD IN FACTORY AND LABORATORIES! BUT WE ALL NEED FOOD, DON'T WE? AND THERE ARE SO MANY HUMAN BEINGS THAT NEED TO BE FED. SEVEN BILLION, TO BE PRECISE.

Absolutely, we need to make enough food for the entire population, but a lot of the crops grown today are not intended for human consumption.

A look at where most of our crop ends up:

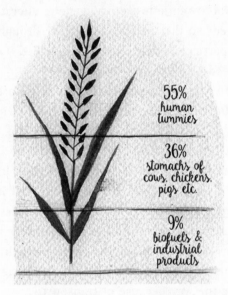

55%
human
tummies

36%
stomachs of
cows. chickens.
pigs etc.

9%
biofuels &
industrial
products

Information source: National Geographic *magazine*[1]

We need to take a closer look at our food system—how we
grow and produce food today and for whom. A lot of the
problem comes from unequal distribution of food. Some
countries and people have more food, and some don't. For
example, if food prices shoot up, rich people can still afford
to eat and buy food. Like say when tur dal and onions
become expensive (it happens often, read the newspaper),
many people can still eat it. But people with less money

---

[1]http://s3.documentcloud.org/documents/1327852/ngm-food-comp-with-ads-
final.pdf

spend most of their income on food. So imagine if the price of dal becomes almost double, then they can't buy it. And dal is a huge source of protein in our country.

From farm to fork

While farmers work hard to grow our food, they don't always get a fair price for the hard work they do to grow our food. A lot of it goes to middle-men and companies, rather than the people who actually grew the food!

Take for example, chocolate. Now if you pay Rs 110 for 100 grams of chocolate, then can you calculate who gets paid what in the food supply chain?

Who	Per cent share	Amount (in rupees and paisa)
The farmer who grows the cacao	6.6	
Transportation and traders	2.1	
Processors and grinders	7.6	
Government	4.3	
Chocolate company	35.2	
Supermarket	44.2	

Source: Make Chocolate Fair

What do you make of this? Farmers get only a small amount of money that we consumers pay for the products we buy. That amount is not enough to make a living. The largest chunk of the money goes to big companies for processing, branding and selling the food. Is that fair? What do you think?

Make way for Rachel Carson

Superheroes save the world from evil villains who are determined to destroy it. But Rachel Carson's modus operandi was way cooler than that. In 1962, she wrote a book called *Silent Spring*, where she talked about the indiscriminate use of chemical pesticides after World War II.

In her book *Silent Spring*, Rachel Carson wrote that DDT, aka dichlorodiphenyltrichloroethane, was one of the pesticides sure to spark a cancer epidemic. It's now a POP (not a rock star, duh) a Persistent Organic Pollutant. It stays put in fatty tissues of the body and can travel long distances. DDT is banned in many countries across the world. India has promised to phase it out by 2020, but we are still using it.!

'Sprays, dusts and aerosols are now applied almost universally to farms, gardens, forests and homes—non-selective chemicals that have the power to kill every insect, the "good" and the "bad", to still the song of the birds and the leaping of fish in the streams, to coat the leaves with a deadly film and to linger on in the soil—all this though the intended target may be only a few weeds or insects,' Rachel Carson wrote in her book.

One year later, Rachel testified before the U.S. Congress, asking for new policies to protect the environment and human health. She is now considered one of the foremost environmental activists of our times.

RACK YOUR BRAINS
Look up more complex pesticide names
and make a tongue twister out of them.
'Deepa douses dichlorodiphenyltrichloroethane
on the dal in the dakshin.'

Does something sound seedy?

Across the world, people are demanding that their food should be labelled if it is genetically modified (GM). One thing is clear—if people are paying money for a product, they should be given the option to choose what they want to eat or wear. But the people who manufacture GM seeds don't want to! For example, over 90 per cent of cotton in India is grown from GM seeds. It's called Bt Cotton and it is resistant to certain pests and gives a good harvest for the first few years.

But GM cotton seeds are expensive, and farmers have to buy a pesticide with it, which is also expensive. Many poor farmers can't buy it, but they have no choice, because often that's what most seed traders are selling in the market. Since they need the seeds, they are forced to borrow money from corrupt moneylenders at ridiculous interest rates. Then they are in debt for really small amounts, and unable to repay the moneylenders if their harvest fails.

There are, thankfully, no known health hazards of eating GM produce so far. However, the pesticide that accompanies the seed often destroys the soil over time. And you know how they say once you harvest a plant, the seed can be sown again? Hybrid or GM seeds can't be replanted, which means farmers have to buy new seeds all over again. Sounds like a waste.

HANG ON A MINUTE, DIDN'T WE ALSO TALK ABOUT HOW AGRICULTURE IS A BIG CONTRIBUTOR TO CLIMATE CHANGE?

Remember the Greenhouse Effect? By now you know that when it comes to contributing to global warming, it's agriculture that emits one-third of greenhouse gases[1]. This includes making fertilizer, storing and packaging food, and clearing land for agriculture. That doesn't mean you use it as an excuse to stop eating your dal-bhaji. Rather, it's got to do with, excuse me, belching cows.

Smelly cow, smelly cow, what are you burping and farting now?

Cows have four stomachs[2], and as they digest their food, there's a lot of methane and carbon dioxide being produced to help the process along. Burps are the way these cows get rid of these ruminal gases.

According to the Penn State College of Agricultural

[1] http://www.nationalgeographic.com/foodfeatures/feeding-9-billion/
[2] http://www.washingtonpost.com/news/energy-environment/wp/2015/07/31/how-cleaner-cow-burps-could-help-fight-climate-change/

Sciences, some 132 to 264-gallon ruminal gas is produced every single day[1]. The FAO[2] estimates that livestock supply chain emits some 44 per cent methane and most of it from burps. There's definitely someone in your family, who after a good meal, belches in satisfaction. Now imagine hundreds and thousands of cattle belching at the same time. Or letting out methane super-powered farts!

Apart from the cattle, farming requires a lot of water, and huge areas of forest land are cleared for agriculture, adding carbon dioxide to the air. That also is a big reason why wildlife is dwindling.

---

[1] http://extension.psu.edu/animals/dairy/nutrition/nutrition-and-feeding/diet-formulation-and-evaluation/carbon-methane-emissions-and-the-dairy-cow

[2] http://www.fao.org/news/story/en/item/197623/icode/

RACK YOUR BRAINS
If you were a scientist, and had to reduce cattle burps, how would you go about it? Researchers are looking at 'backpacks' to collect burps, for one solution. Others say cows that eat healthier food burp less. Can you think of a way to add less gaseous burps to the atmosphere?

_____

_____

_____

_____

Postcard from Stephanie Weiss
A world without chocolate, can you imagine?

Stephy, as she prefers to be called, is a food adventurer from Bolivia. Here, she tells you about one of her favourite foods, chocolate. She believes a lot of problems can be solved by eating chocolate. But not just any chocolate.

Did you know that the main ingredient to make chocolate is taken from cacao seeds? These seeds are first fermented and dried to make cocoa liquor, butter and powder.

The place of origin of cacao is still debated. Genetic studies have demonstrated that the origin of the cacao is from the Latin American Amazonia.

Considered the 'food of the gods' by the ancient Mayas—in what today we know as Mexico and Guatemala in Central

America—this crop needs certain conditions of sunshine, altitude and humidity to grow. That is why you will mostly find them growing near the Equator line. Today, most of the cacao is produced and exported from Ivory Coast in Africa. Together with Ghana, Nigeria and Cameroon they produce 70 per cent of the cacao consumed worldwide.

Cacao is still produced in South America today. Bolivian cacao, the country from where I am, is special. That's because it is planted in the southern-most part of the continent and at a higher altitude than most cacao plantations around the world. Experts say this has provided Bolivian cacao with a special differentiation. In 2015, the cacao from the northern part of the Bolivian Amazon was ranked among the best cacao of the world.

Even though cacao was successfully adapted to different parts of the world, it is under great risk! It is threatened by pests, fungal infections and climate change. Because of climate change, rain fed crops in Africa, as in other parts of the world, could reduce by half by the year 2020! Let's not forget that even though you can eat and divide chocolate bars into equal pieces, the world of chocolate is still not fair. Many of the people that plant and harvest the cacao have never even tasted chocolate! They are paid poorly for hard work in extreme weather conditions. Most of the cacao leaves the countries of production to be processed abroad in Europe and other parts of the world, and this way most of the earnings do not reach the workers. Next time you eat chocolate, check the labels and try to see if you can find out where the cacao comes from... good luck!

SO MANY PROBLEMS IN FARMING! WHAT CAN WE DO TO SUPPORT OUR FARMERS?

Fewer and fewer farmers want to stay in agriculture in India. And who can blame them? They don't get good prices for their produce, farming is hard work—it's back breaking, imagine plucking cotton all day—seeds and fertilizers are expensive, and there's little protection against climate change. But we still need food, don't we? And we depend on farmers to grow that!

As people who live in cities, we can do plenty!

▶ Find out where your food comes from: Talk to your vegetable vendor or supermarket manager and ask them to ensure their food is sourced responsibly.

▶ When possible, buy produce straight from farmers. A lot of cities now have real farmers' markets where they invite farmers to come and sell produce.

▶ Grow your own food on your window sill, balcony or terrace. Tomatoes, herbs, root vegetables grow very easily and taste yummier if you've grown them yourself.

▶ Oh come on, we don't have all the answers. You come up with some as well.

_____

_____

_____

_____

Fresh from the field

Move over Old MacDonald who had a farm, e-i-e-i-o.

It's time to meet some real, happy farmers who are growing organic, diverse, and fairly-traded produce, e-i-e-i-yo.

Visit a seed fest

Every year, farmers gather across different parts of the country to exhibit and exchange their local seeds at seed fests. For instance, at the Fair Trade Alliance Kerala's (FTAK) annual seed fest, farmers come from four districts of Kerala and set up stalls to display their seeds.

When I visited the seed fest in 2015, I met one farmer who had come from the Wayanad district where he grows twenty-six kinds of chillies. Sunni, another organic farmer said that since 2005 he had switched to organic farming, and now his personal health had improved. Shobhana

Ravi is also from Wayanad and said by participating in such events she has become more confident as a woman farmer.

According to the FTAK co-founder Tomy Mathew, the farmers come together not only to exchange local and organic seeds, but as a form of climate adaptation. Farmers preserve local varieties of seeds that are native to Kerala, which means they don't need to buy expensive ones from seed companies. Alongside their cash crops of cashewnuts, coconut and coffee, they grow potato, brinjal, chillies, peas and fruits so that they have enough food at all times to eat.

The farmers don't believe in growing only one plant variety (that's called mono cropping). Instead they grow everything together, which is good for the soil and does not deplete it of nutrients. The excess food they grow they sell in the market. That way, even if their crop fails because of an erratic monsoon, they have food to eat, even if they have lesser money.

A bank of seeds

Nabita Goud is a farmer and a banker in Bhimdanga village in Odisha's Kalahandi district. Confused? That's because she actually manages a seed bank in her village. Nabita is a Seed Guardian at the Maa Lankeshwari Seed Bank and is one of eighteen Seed Guardians who are part of Chetna Organic's seed conservation project in five villages in Odisha. Seed banks, like the one she manages, conserve a variety of seeds.

A seed bank operates just like a bank! A farmer can 'withdraw' a kilo of seed and has to repay the loan with one-and-a-half kilo of seed after harvest. How cool is that? In India, farmers traditionally saved their seeds to sow after every harvest.

Nabita's seed bank is in a small room inside a hut. It's lined with rows of neatly labelled earthen pots and jars to protect them from climatic conditions. There are varieties of millets, ladies finger, pumpkin, and red gram seeds, along with cotton. Nabita and her neighbours don't need to buy expensive seeds from the market anymore. And all because of this community effort!

❓ Huh fact of the day

There's a seed bank in the Arctic called the Svalvard Global Seed Vault and it stores over 8,30,000 varieties of seeds from almost every country in the world. Recently, scientists made a withdrawal from the seed bank to retrieve precious wheat, barley, and grasses seeds (that's because of the civil war going on in Syria). They have a very cool website where you can make a virtual visit of the vault. Check out *https://www.croptrust.org/what-we-do/ svalbard-global-seed-vault/*.

IS THERE A WAY TO KNOW WHO GREW OUR FOOD AND WHERE IT CAME FROM?

Sometimes you buy a packet of tea, coffee or chocolate and it has a label of certification by Fairtrade or Rainforest Alliance, or by UTZ, which is an organic body.

It means that the product has ingredients sourced from a farm which met certain social, environmental, and economic criteria and was checked by these certification agencies. It often tells you where the food was grown as well.

For example, when you see the Fairtrade Mark, it means that the farmers got paid a fair price for their produce (most of the time they don't, unfortunately) and they got an extra amount of money called the Fairtrade Premium to invest back in their farms or communities. Fairtrade also has strict standards to help prevent environmental abuse, human trafficking, child labour and forced labour.

The Rainforest Alliance seal shows that those farms and forests, from which the ingredients came from, met environmental, social and economic standards.

Organic means that no pesticide was used while growing the produce.

It's all about a clean, good supply chain—from farm to table.

APART FROM PESTICIDES, OUR FOOD SYSTEM IS GETTING MORE AND PROCESSED. UMMM, SO WHAT EXACTLY ARE PROCESSED FOODS?

Food processing is done to prevent food from going bad at a natural pace. We have always treated food to various processes at home to preserve them—think about pickling raw mango or lemons so that they can stay edible for a long time, or how the Egyptians cured fish with salt so they could carry it on their long journeys.

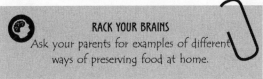

RACK YOUR BRAINS
Ask your parents for examples of different ways of preserving food at home.

When industrial food processing was introduced, it caught on fast. It also helped transport food during war time to serve military needs. After the war ended, the practice caught on fast with civilians, too. Canned tomatoes, milk in tetra packs, yoghurt in shiny containers with a not-easy-to-peel-away-despite-what-the-manufacturers-claim lid, what's not to love?

Today, a lot of the processing involves refined ingredients which are not very nutritious or they have added chemicals. Processed foods often add salt, sugar or fat, all those yummy things your taste buds loves but are pretty bad for your body. Does that mean you give up everything you like? No! For example, French fries made fresh at home are better for you than the ones that come out of a frozen packet.

> ## ⸮Chew on this
>
> Azodicarbonamide may sound like a complex spell, destined to confound young potion makers, or like someone just sneezed. But it's the name of an additive that manufacturers add to bread to make it look whiter. Food activist Vani Hari, who lives in North Carolina, pointed out that the same additive is used to make yoga mats and can be problematic for humans. Yikes!

Become a label decoder

While buying something processed or packaged, you need to know the ingredients. After all, it's going into your tummy. For that, you need to become a Label Decoder.

The small print on the back of a food packet tells you a lot about what ingredients it is made out of. They are often confusing and read like Greek or Latin. But no worries, there is a way of understanding the meaning behind a food label.

Look at a label—it can be of a biscuit or chips packet or a chocolate wrapper. Now divide the ingredients into two parts. You may need to use the Internet to figure some of the names out.

Ingredients	From a Farm	From a Lab

So how much of your food was grown in a farm or created in a lab?

_____
_____
_____
_____
_____
_____
_____
_____
_____

⚘ Chew on this

How many ingredients does your morning breakfast cereal have, or your afternoon cookie? In comparison, how many ingredients does your yoghurt or homemade nankhatai have? Would it be difficult to eat food that have five or less processed ingredients?

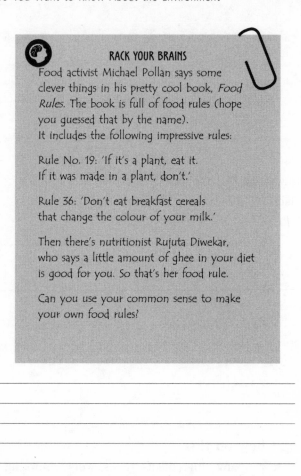

RACK YOUR BRAINS

Food activist Michael Pollan says some clever things in his pretty cool book, *Food Rules*. The book is full of food rules (hope you guessed that by the name).
It includes the following impressive rules:

Rule No. 19: 'If it's a plant, eat it.
If it was made in a plant, don't.'

Rule 36: 'Don't eat breakfast cereals that change the colour of your milk.'

Then there's nutritionist Rujuta Diwekar, who says a little amount of ghee in your diet is good for you. So that's her food rule.

Can you use your common sense to make your own food rules?

TO DO OR NOT TO DO, THAT'S REALLY UP TO YOU

ACTION 1
Take a Food Survey

Conduct a food survey of your friends and family to find out what they eat. After all, you are what you eat.

Identify friends and family members who fall in the following age groups:

80+: Super Senior

60+: Senior

35+: Middle-aged

25+: Not-so-young

Your age and +: Young

They could be in the same city or in different parts of India, or even abroad. In fact, the more diverse your sample size (the number of people you interview are called samples!), the more interesting your answers.

Interview people from each group to learn about their food habits.

You can ask questions such as:

What kind of food did they eat while growing up?

_____

_____

What was a usual meal when they were growing up? Ask about breakfast, lunch, tea, and dinner.

_____

_____

Was dessert an everyday occurrence or was it a treat for special occasions?

_____

_____

What was their idea of a splendid meal?

_____

_____

Where did they eat most of their meals?

_____

_____

How have their eating habits changed over the years?

_____

_____

What kind of food/lifestyle-related illnesses were common as they grew up? Have those changed over time?

_____

_____

Did they get seasonal fruits and vegetables only during seasons or through the year?

_____

_____

Come up with your own questions now. Don't be lazy.

_____

_____

Now compare the answers with each age group. Are there any huge differences in diet (you have to think like a scientist, so talk like one too)? Were food habits simpler back then, or now? Could you identify any trend right now for food—like Italian cuisine or cupcakes? Were the answers what you expected or were there any surprises in there?

ACTION 2
Make a Food Map of your kitchen

Your house is most probably a sum of the entire world.

Okay, that's a confusing line.

Today, with food travelling across countries, it's as easy to buy a kiwi from Australia, as it is to get spinach from your local farmer. There's a term for this—Food Miles. It is the distance your food travels—from the time it's grown, to the factory where it is processed and packed, and then shipped to the final consumer, that is you. Transportation burns a lot of fossil fuel, causing a lot of pollution because of the distance it has travelled—by plane, road, rail, and even ship.

How do you figure out how much your food has travelled to come to your kitchen? Start by calculating the miles, or in our case kilometres, that each food item has travelled.

To make it a less crazy task, choose five categories such as fruits, dry fruits, chocolates, vegetables, dairy etc.

Include place of origin—that is where it was grown. For chocolate, it could be that the cacao was grown in Ghana. Next, it went to Switzerland for processing to be made into chocolate at a chocolate factory. Then, it was packaged and shipped across to Mumbai to be sold. If you're wondering where to look for this information, for packaged food items, look at the label—it includes details of the manufacturing process.

If it's a perishable food such as potato or strawberry, you will need to ask your vegetable or fruit seller where it comes from.

Name of food item	Perishable/ Non-perishable	Origin	Processing	Distance travelled from place of origin to your house (km)
Potato	Perishable	Pune		150
Quinoa	Non-perishable	Bolivia		15,394
Chocolate	Non-perishable	Ghana	Switzerland	6,190 (Ghana to Switzerland) +11,290 = 17,480

Cheat tip: Visit *http://www.foodmiles.com/* to calculate the miles of your food in a jiffy. It even gives you fun facts about the sort of transportation that was used to transport your food and how much carbon would that create.

Once you have your food miles calculated, plot these onto a world map. Connect each point with lines, and get a world view of how much your food has travelled. Talk about jet lag.

Not all food miles are bad. Say, something is grown sustainably in a far-away country—tomatoes grow in Maharashtra in open fields, which means they use less carbon as compared to tomatoes grown in Sweden. Why is that? Because those tomatoes are grown in greenhouses, which are heated by fossil fuels and they need a lot of fertilizers that release nitrogen oxide in the air. Then it's possible that it's better for the Swedes to get tomatoes from India.

ACTION 3
Food forms

When rice is cooked at home, it becomes this fragrant bowl of long strands of white rice. But before that, it's a kind of paddy! It has to be processed before it looks like the rice we eat.

Paddy

Harvested stalks

Threshing

Brown Rice

Drying and hulling

Can you trace the process from seed to edible food for some of your favourite food items? You can use the table for reference or make a drawing of the stages of processing to understand how your food has changed or kept its form.

Crop	Plant	Harvested	Processing Step 1	Processing Step 2	To my home
Tomato					Ketchup
Cacao					Chocolate
Vanilla					Cake
Wheat					Chapati
Sugarcane					Cookies
Potato					Fries

Some foods will have less processing steps—such as potatoes if you're making fries at home. But if you're buying frozen fries from the supermarket, that will add many more steps.

ACTION 4
A veggie for each season

If you have done Action I, then you may already know that in The Days of Yore, your grandparents used to eat food according to the season.

My grandmother, for one, would look forward to winter. That's because it was an excuse to layer up on ghee-laden foods such as godpapdi, which is a barfi-like sweet dish with jaggery and wheat flour. It isn't really suitable for summers because it's too hot then.

For my mother, summers were reserved for pouring watermelon juice in ice trays and making them into sorbets, before sorbet became gourmet ice cream parlour foods. And mum just refuses to eat spinach during the monsoon because she says they are full of worms and germs.

Similarly, a lot of people don't eat fish during the rainy season because it's breeding time for the fish and that's when they are best left alone.

See, more food rules!

Reason seasonal foods[1] rock:

- Vegetables and fruits are most flavourful during the right season. Alphonso mangoes are best eaten in May. Those that appear in March are not that sweet or tasty.

- If you're eating seasonal produce, it's most probably locally grown and you're supporting local farmers. For instance, eating strawberries from Mahabaleshwar during winter or purple, squishy jamuns as the monsoon sets in.

- Some people ripen bananas[2] artificially with scary, harmful

---

[1]http://www.theguardian.com/lifeandstyle/wordofmouth/2014/aug/12/seasonal-eating-vegetables-uk-does-it-matter

[2]http://www.fssai.gov.in/Portals/0/Pdf/Article_on_fruits.pdf

chemicals such as calcium carbide to make sure it's available around the year. It's simpler to eat it when it is in season.

• Fruits and veggies are cheaper when they are available seasonally.

Can you make up a seasonal food calendar? Talk to a farmer, to grandparents, veggie seller, and make a list of edibles according to the season and the place you live.

Seasonal Calendar

You can make a colourful calendar and put it up on the fridge.

When it's hot, good to eat:

_____

_____

But avoid:

_____

_____

When it's cold, good to eat:

_____

_____

But avoid:

_____

_____

When it's raining, good to eat:

_____

_____

But avoid:

_____

_____

ACTION 5
Start a Sniff Diary

All said and done, food is about taste. If it doesn't taste good, you just won't eat it. Unless your parents make you, because it is good for you. Of course, everyone has different food tastes—some like those bitter karelas, some the squelchy laukis and others can't stand stringy bhindi.

For long, scientists thought there were four tastes, and then came along Umami—a pleasant, savoury taste that can come from shiitake mushrooms, fermented fish, meats, and Marmite. Can you think of foods that taste the following?

Type	Example
Sweet	
Sour	
Salty	
Bitter	
Umami	

To taste food, and truly appreciate it, you need to use your senses. Ever seen a professional chef at work? They don't cook by taste alone. That would be quite horrid, them dipping a finger into your food all the time. Rather they use their sense of touch, smell and sight to improvise a recipe. In fact, a study conducted by the Taste and Smell Clinic at the University of Pennsylvania Hospital showed that people without the sense of smell had problems cooking and eating[1].

---

[1] *Season to Taste*: Molly Birnbaum, Portobello Books

Anosmia is the inability to perceive smells. Imagine not being to smell someone farting (a good thing) or eating a piece of stale bread but not able to make that out, because you can't smell it (not good).

When was the last time you distinctly remember smelling something apart from polluting fumes, petrol and paint?

The sense of smell is a powerful one, as much as the sense of taste, sight and sound. But as you grow older, your olfactory (smelling) powers start to reduce. But you can exercise your sense of smell! Here are a few experiments to get you sniffing away.

🍎

EXPERIMENT 1
Blind man's bluff

Enlist the help of a friend, adult, or sibling. Take turns to blindfold each other, and hold food items in front of the respective noses. Smell different kinds of food (throw in non-food items to confuse each other) and try to identify them. Here are a few suggestions:

- Bulb of garlic
- Onion
- Strong cheese
- Saffron
- Chocolate
- Tea
- Coffee
- Pencil shavings
- An old book

- Add your own item

How many items can you identify just by smelling them?

·

EXPERIMENT 2

The Pinch-Your-Nose experiment

Close your nose and eat different food items and see if you can taste them. Some of you may already do that with milk—pinch your nose and drink it. If you can't smell it, then you can't taste it!

- Chocolate
- Hot chocolate
- Biryani
- Cooked bhindi
- Milk
- Again, make up your own list.

Do the same experiment but by taking a deep breath and actually inhaling the smell of that food before taking a bite.

Was there any difference?

·

EXPERIMENT 3

Nirmal Kulkarni is a herpetologist in Goa, which means he spends a lot of time in the forest studying amphibians like frogs and reptiles such as snakes. Nirmal says that every forest smells different at different times and every river too. Go on, dare you to go around sniffing forests and rivers at different times of the day (never alone) to see how they smell.

He insists that if you smell a flower once, you will always remember that smell. In fact, he says that in the forest, tigers sometimes smell like ground garlic! How pungent they must be!

Nirmal clearly has a good nose, and you can have one too. Start a Sniff Diary and actually record strange, comforting, pleasant and ugh smells in the diary.

WASTE

where do you
think all our
waste goes?

WASTE SIDE STORY

Deepanjana was thrilled to be moving into a new house. It was one of those houses which had rainwater harvesting and greywater recycling facilities. She marvelled at the solar water heater and beamed at her recycle bins. There were three of them—Wet Waste, Dry Waste, and Other Waste. Deepanjana was keen to start recycling so that she would be responsible for less waste filling up landfills.

> Next day, being Saturday, DJ (seriously, Deepanjana is a long name) was preparing a sandwich.
> She hoped to recycle all the waste, without a hitch.
> Off went the plastic bread wrapper, banished into Dry Waste.
> The lettuce ends were neatly snipped off and chucked into Wet Waste, along with the ends of the purple onions, tomatoes, and fish paste.
> An egg was scrambled, and DJ wondered which bin would the shells go in,
> The Wet Bin, the Dry Bin, or in the Other Bin?
> Her portable radio's battery died out, and she dithered between putting them in either Dry or Other.
> Just then her cat pooped, and she wondered if cat poop get composted? Oh, what a bother!
> Oh my! Oh my! This isn't as easy as it did look...
> DJ had to find out how to recycle, by hook or by crook.

Recycling mantra

That was a terrible rhyme. But it did not stink as much

(alright maybe it did) as our world's garbage problems. And not all of them can get sorted out by recycling. But, recycling can help to some extent.

So, let's start from the very beginning.
The very beginning we start.
When you sing you begin with Do Re Me...
When you bin,
You begin with Refuse, Reuse, Recycle, Reduce.

See how it's easy to remember?
No? Okay, back to Deepanjana who is desperately texting her friend, Lalitha to figure out how to reduce waste.

Deepanjana: Seriously, my garbage bins, all three of them are overflowing. What do I do?

Lalitha: It's simple, DJ. You Refuse, Reuse, Recycle, Reduce.

Deepanjana: Hang on, those are 4 Rs!

Lalitha: Yes, so?

Deepanjana: There have always been 3 Rs of recycling—Reuse, Recycle, and Reduce.

Lalitha: Yes, and now there's one more—Refuse.

Deepanjana: What for? I don't understand.

Sigh. Explanation follows for Deepanjana and everyone.

THE BIG GARBAGE PROBLEM

Get up now, er...don't forget to take this book with you. Walk into your kitchen and look at the trash. Is it overflowing?

It is, isn't it?

Where did all that trash come from?

If you look closely, okay don't get too close. Like, don't jump in. But if you were to spend a day observing your house habits when it comes to trash, you will figure that we are generating tons of it, from:

▶ Food peels
▶ Food packaging
▶ Paper waste
▶ Plastic waste
▶ Courier packaging
▶ Candy wrappers
▶ Toy packaging
▶ Leftover food
▶ Old electronics such as batteries and cords

Add below the names of the other things you found in your trash can.

_____

_____

_____

_____

All this stuff takes time to break down. Here's a timeline[1]:

Glass Bottle	1 million years
Plastic Bottles	450 years
Disposable Diapers	450 years
Aluminium Can	80-200 years
Foamed Plastic Cups	50 years
Rubber-Boot Sole	50-80 years
Tin Cans	50 years
Leather	50 years
Nylon Fabric	30-40 years
Plastic Bag	10-20 years
Cigarette Butt	1-5 years
Plywood	1-3 years
Waxed Milk Carton	3 months
Apple Core	2 months
Newspaper	6 weeks
Orange or Banana Peel	2-5 weeks
Paper Towel	2-4 weeks

RACK YOUR BRAINS
Create a graph of your dustbin—trash on one side, and the amount of time it takes to decompose on the other side.

[1]http://des.nh.gov/organization/divisions/water/wmb/coastal/trash/documents/marine_debris.pdf

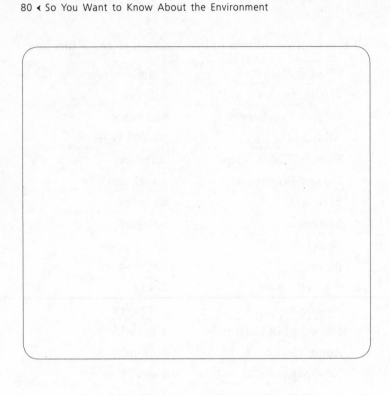

WHAT'S INSIDE OUR COUNTRY'S DUSTBIN?

Now that you know what your household trash looks like, multiply that by everyone who lives in your building, your school, your area. Then think about hospitals, factories, shopping complexes—how much waste is being generated across the world?

Every year, we generate 42 million tons of waste[1]! The world is chucking two billion tons every day. And we

---

[1] http://www.chintan-india.org/documents/fact_sheets/chintan_waste_tales_fact_sheet.pdf

need more and more land to dump this trash somewhere.

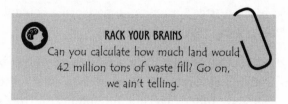

RACK YOUR BRAINS
Can you calculate how much land would 42 million tons of waste fill? Go on, we ain't telling.

Here's what constitutes waste:

▸ **Domestic waste:** From cooking, cleaning to food packaging, stationery etc.
▸ **Industrial waste:** From factories, industries, tanneries etc.
▸ **Municipal waste:** All the stuff from your house is carted away by the municipality. Apart from the trash generated from the roads and elsewhere across the city.
▸ **Institutional waste:** From schools, colleges, hospitals.
▸ **Commercial waste:** From offices, stores, markets, restaurants.
▸ **Building waste:** From construction sites.

Some of this waste is biodegradable, which means it can be broken down by bacteria. Some cannot be decomposed, and some of it can be recycled in parts (more about that in a bit).

And the 'Biggest Trash Culprit Award' goes to...

Delhi. The city generates 8,000 metric tons every single day.

But if you are sitting back and saying, phew, I don't live in Delhi, wait. Turns out, some 72 per cent waste is generated by the seven big cities in India.

Aiyo! So much waste. But we are a developing country, we cannot be wasting that much!

According to the World Bank[1], worldwide three billion urban residents generate 1.2 kg municipal solid waste per person per day. India may not be among the top waste generators, but our waste generation is expected to triple[2] by 2025. Which means, we do need to spruce up our waste management systems (apart from wasting less).

Let's take the example of a ballpoint pen. Ask your parents or grandparents, and they will tell you that as a child, there was a special joy in being afforded the privilege to use a ballpoint pen. And when the pen's ink got used up, it meant a trip to the stationery store to carefully choose the right refill for it.

When did you last refill your pen? (Don't tell me that you don't use one because all your homework is done on your super-smart tablet!) Or did you 'use-and-throw' it away

[1]http://web.worldbank.org/WBSITE/EXTERNAL/TOPICS/EXTURBANDEVE
LOPMENT/0,,contentMDK:23172887~pagePK:210058~piPK:210062~theSite
PK:337178,00.html
[2]http://www.livemint.com/Politics/XsXf3cmvKjaoHPnlo31Y0H/South-Asia-to-
become-fastest-waste-producer-by-2025.html

after it stopped working?

Pens are cheaper, and that means it's easier to buy a new one—and there are so many cool pens in the market now.

An average ballpoint pen is made up of plastic or metal with a plastic refill, all of which are difficult to recycle. According to a study[1], the Indian market 'for writing pens is 1,600–2,400 million pieces per year'. If you were to stay on the conservative side, we are using approximately 4,444,444 pens per day. And at least, 70 per cent of pen sales in India is that of ballpoint ones. Just imagine a landfill full of mountains of pens. And this is just one example—of a tiny pen!

RACK YOUR BRAINS

How would you cut down the number of pens that go in a landfill? Use fountain pens that can be refilled, buy lesser pens, use a pen until its ink runs out or your desk partner nabs it, recycle it, or upcycle it into a piece of art? Put on your thinking caps and pen some thoughts.

Hint: It all comes down to our HABITS.

---

[1]http://www.niir.org/profiles/profiles/stationery-stationery-products-pens-pencils-ink-pads-staplers-glue-pen-pencil-boxes-geometry-sets-desk-accessories-exercise-note-book-files-school-stationery-office-stationery-writing-instruments-envelope-all-pin-ball-pen-refills/z,,7b,0,a/index.html

PLASTIC—NOT YUM FOR ANIMALS AND MARINE LIFE

Ever seen a cow rooting about in garbage? Chances are that she will end up eating plastic from the garbage, and it will stay in her stomach, ultimately killing her. And plastic also chokes up marine life and other animals and birds.

And it's not just land that's becoming a dustbin. Fancy a swim in the Great Pacific Garbage Patch?

A lot of trash doesn't end up in the landfill, instead it's sent off to sea! And then it becomes 'Not Our Problem'.

Unfortunately, stuff like plastic isn't always biodegradable, and it gets swept up by an ocean gyre—a system of circular ocean currents because of the wind and the Earth's rotation—and becomes part of a swirling trash vortex. The chemicals in the plastic break down over time and can be dangerous for aquatic life.

The biggest trash vortex is in the Great Pacific—it is roughly twice the size of Texas, but there are trash vortexes in the Indian and Atlantic Oceans as well. The United Nations Environment Program[1] estimated 18,000 pieces of floating plastic in every square km of the ocean. And that was way back in 2006.

There are lots of solutions being discussed—scientists are suggesting placement of plastic collectors by coasts; a nineteen-year-old boy (back in 2014) is testing floating

---

[1] http://www.unep.org/regionalseas/marinelitter/publications/docs/plastic_ocean_report.pdf

barriers and platforms to collect the plastic from the water; and of course, environmentalists are suggesting we stop dumping plastic in the ocean.

SO, WE ARE IN TROUBLE. EITHER RISING SEA LEVEL IS GOING TO DROWN US, WHERE WE WILL BE BOBBING ALONGSIDE TONS OF PLASTIC WATER BOTTLES, OR OUR WASTE IS GOING TO SWALLOW US UP. THANKS, GROWN-UPS, WELL-DONE WITH THE WORLD.

Calm down. It does look difficult. But there's plenty you can do to get adults to clean up their act. Start by working on the 4 Rs. When segregating garbage, it means doing what DJ was trying to accomplish—putting the right waste in the correct bin so it's easy to recycle. If your local municipality doesn't support waste separation, then get together with your community to start it at each house and start vermicomposting with the entire locality.

RACK YOUR BRAINS
How many trash-related puns can you think of? There's two in this section already (the rhyme stinks and get adults to clean up their act). What more can you come up with?

_____
_____
_____
_____
_____
_____
_____
_____

WHAT ROT!

When fruits and vegetables get old, they start to rot. Ever seen an apple shrivel up and look like an old person's skin? And when fleas start swarming on days-old bananas, until they become all black and yucky? That's called rotting. When animals and plants rot, they become humus (dark organic matter), which is good for the soil.

That's nature's very own recycling plant, where she makes sure nothing goes to waste.

Do you always eat only when you're hungry? No, right?

Unlike us, animals only eat when they are hungry. For example, the tiger, who is a predator, once he is done the hyenas and vultures eat the rest of the carcass. They are called scavengers. Then, the bacteria and fungi take over to break it down completely.

In the forest, the leaves of the trees fall down into the soil. Microorganisms take over—such as bacteria, fungi, algae, and plankton—they help decompose matter and turn it back into soil. See, zero waste cycle!

Say hello to the farmer's friend and even yours: the earthworm.

Earthworms may look icky, but they are one of the most important, well, worms on the planet. They munch on soil and organic matter, and poop it out as broken down stuff. They also wriggle through the soil, making tunnels, which in turn helps oxygen get deep into the soil and also lets excess water drain off.

Try this
Go to a nearby garden where lots of plants are growing. Pick up a bit of soil and press it in your hands and smell it. If it's loose, crumbly, and smells like the Earth, that's good soil.

Erm... why... are we talking about worms?

Coming back to the waste issue at hand. When things rot, we also call them compost and when you get worms to help you compost, it becomes vermicomposting. And we can help reduce the landfill and trash vortex problem by composting at home, in our colony, school, or somewhere close by.

You need to start sorting your garbage, just like DJ did in the beginning of this section. Segregation at home means it won't get mixed up in the landfills and contaminate water or release methane (that's right, another GHG). It also helps rag pickers who otherwise sort trash by hand and face health hazards.

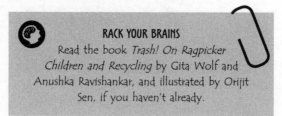

RACK YOUR BRAINS
Read the book *Trash! On Ragpicker Children and Recycling* by Gita Wolf and Anushka Ravishankar, and illustrated by Orijit Sen, if you haven't already.

BECOME A COM-POST MAN OR WOMAN

Before you begin segregating your trash, you need to know your garbage in and out. Here are a few tips.

Wet waste is stuff you can compost. This is organic waste and it can be converted into compost, which is also known as Black Gold. Waste managers believe that almost 60–65 per cent of our everyday waste can be composted!

Dry waste you send for recycling because it takes time to break down. It needs to be handled by recyclers and counts for almost 30 per cent of our waste.

Other or rejects waste is the waste that cannot be decomposed, recycled, or reused.

Wet Waste	Dry Waste	Other Waste
Foods	Paper	Medicines
Plants	Plastic	Batteries
Coffee	Glass	E-waste
Tea	Thermocol	Sanitary waste
Food paper such as pizza boxes or tissues	Tetra Pak	Cat poop
Disposable paper bags and cups	Fabric	
Pencil shavings	Coconut husk	
Egg shells		

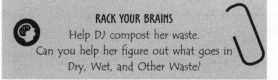

RACK YOUR BRAINS
Help DJ compost her waste.
Can you help her figure out what goes in
Dry, Wet, and Other Waste?

Cheat sheet: Head to *www.dailydump.org* to get your own vermicomposting kit.

Postcard from Shailaja Rangarajan
The Tetra Pak trail

Shailaja gives Trash Talks to people in Bengaluru and tells them how to manage their waste better. In fact, she says you will find her wherever there's trash! They are like portkeys for her.

What happens once you bin that juice carton, which is called a Tetra Pak, after drinking it? This is what happens in India. When you're done with your juice carton, you bin it. It gets carted off by the garbage truck and gets to a landfill.

Rag pickers collect Tetra Pak like these and sell them to waste aggregators, who specialise in certain kind of trash.

The aggregators sell it on to recyclers. The cartons are squashed and put together into bundles. One carton has six layers which are made out of Paperboard (75 per cent), polyethylene, and aluminium[1].

The bundles are put into a pulp machine with water and converted into pulp. Recycling starts with separating the paper (which constitutes around 75 per cent of the content) from the plastic and aluminium. Paper can then get recycled into other products.

Plastic and aluminium can be recycled to create roof tiles, pots and even furniture. In Europe in 2007, 33 per cent of all drink cartons were used to generate electricity!

---

[1] http://www.protectswhatsgood.in/about-us/6-layer-protection/

There are groups that give jobs to women who make interesting products such as bags with Tetra Pak.

We can all do simple things. Garbage is everyone's problem. Get your hands dirty and clean it up.

- *Don't buy a bottle of water when you go out.*
- *Buy smart: Instead of a liquid shower gel which has polluting microbeads and comes in a plastic bottle, get an eco-friendly, hand-made soap which won't have harmful chemicals. This saves on packaging too.*
- *Don't litter. If you eat a snack, stow away the packet in your bag to throw when at home in a bin, and not on the road.*
- *Segregate waste at source.*
- *Set up composting in school.*
- *Throw a zero-waste birthday party.*
- *Add your own ideas.*

_____

_____

_____

_____

_____

IT'S TIME TO ADD ANOTHER R: REFUSE/ RECONSIDER

Segregation is not the complete solution. We also need reduce buying things we don't need, not waste things reuse them instead. When it comes to buying thing should use responsibly and recycle it.

Have you ever bought a book or toy from a website? How was it packed? A friend got a slim picture book inside a giant box of 15x15 inches along with tons of bubble wrap. Such a waste of bubble wrap, given it could have come in a simple envelope.

A lot of packaging is necessary to keep things from spoiling. But increasingly, a lot of packaging is unnecessary and wasteful. When shopping, reconsider products that have too much packaging or are 'disposable'. In fact, you will see that when you go to an open vegetable market, you will have less plastic than a supermarket. Most of those retail stores insist on wrapping each piece of vegetable you buy in plastic to be able to tag the produce with a price.

Reconsider your choices. Instead of a plastic or thermocol plate, get one that's made out of dried leaves. Or use a real plate and wash it.

So basically, Reconsider. Or Refuse to buy things that are wasteful.

The cleanest country award goes to... Iceland.

A close second is Sweden which recycles 47 per cent of its waste and 52 per cent is used to generate heat in some 950,000 houses. Less than 1 per cent garbage ends up in the landfill. In fact, they are so good at recycling that they are considering importing waste from other countries for their energy requirements. Talk about zero waste.

EEEE-WASTE

Pop question:

What does Wall-E in *Wall-E* (the Disney Pixar film) stand for?

Answer: As Google must have told you by now, it's an acronym for Waste Allocation Load Lifter—Earth Class.

Wall-E is a trash-compacting robot who lives in an Earth full of garbage and trash. The film makes you think about how greedy human beings can be by just consuming more than they need.

There are plenty of people today who have a very puzzling habit. They buy a smartphone, a tablet, an e-reader, a computer or a TV, and love it.

Then a new smartphone, tablet, e-reader, computer or TV model hits the market.

These weird people then chuck their perfectly good smartphone, tablet, e-reader, computer or TV model and buy the new version.

Ctrl+Repeat Maximus Stupidous Behaviour.

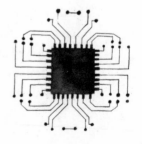

How weird is that?

Worse, manufacturers make their gadgets obsolete by adding upgrades and make you throw them away because they become so slow (the gadgets, not the people), or change the chargers or small things so that you can't reuse them. That's bad design.

Manufacturing gadgets takes a lot of resources from the Earth such as metal and also uses up a lot of energy. Raw materials are mined, and thousands of them are shipped from different parts of the world to a factory to be made into a smartphone, tablet, e-reader, computer or TV, then packaged and shipped to be sold.

E-waste can be hazardous with harmful health and environmental effects. They leach out toxins into the land and atmosphere. According to Greenpeace[1], often e-waste collection is done by workers, including children who don't wear protective gear and are exposed to hazardous chemicals and toxins.

There's plenty that can be done—companies should take back their products and recycle them safely, they should make eco-friendly gadgets that don't go obsolete quickly, we should use products longer or pass them on to people who will use them, and rich countries should take responsibility for their own e-waste, rather than send it for recycling to countries like India, China and Nigeria.

?Huh fact of the day!

Greenpeace found that some 25,000 workers are employed at scrap yards in Delhi, where 10-20,000 tonnes of e-waste is handled each year. And a quarter of this e-waste was computers.

---

[1]http://www.greenpeace.org/international/en/news/features/poisoning-the-poor-electroni/

WHAT DO GORILLAS AND GADGETS HAVE IN COMMON? EXCEPT THE FACT THAT THEIR NAMES START WITH A 'G'.

Imagine that you are a gorilla in East Congo. Go on, it would be awesome to be six feet tall, weigh 200 kilos, and less awesome, that you're an endangered species. You're smart, you have great tracts of forest land to chill in, you can climb trees like, well, a monkey. As a gorilla, you don't use smartphones. You have better things to do with your time, such as pounding your chest, munching on fruits, and mostly hanging about.

Unfortunately for you, humans do use smartphones (and also laptops, tablets and gadgets). And now you and your family are losing your home because of that gadget. Why? People are mining for coltan, short for Columbite-tantalite, a metallic ore found in East Congo. Coltan is an important part of cell phones, laptops and other gadgets because when it is refined, it gets transformed into tantalum, which is heat-resistant and stores energy.

In the Kahuzi Biega National Park, gorilla populations have almost halved because forest land has been cleared for mining. How much does a grown-up pay for a cell phone— ask them. Rs 25,000 to Rs 50,000? Now that phone can't work without coltan, yet miners who mine coltan get paid poorly. It's also often smuggled from Congo, and the profit from it helps fuel war by neighbouring countries.

Ask your tech company to use coltan only from legitimately mined sources. We need Gorilla-Safe Cell Phones!

P.S.: Check out Fairphones, these are smartphones that try to source minerals from conflict-free zones and are built in a way to last longer. Their workers get a fair wage and decent working conditions and the manufacturers offer safe recycling options. How cool is that?

RACK YOUR BRAINS

Hatch a cunning plan to save the gorilla. Make a poster to show the problems with coltan mining, our greed for new and shiny gadgets, the problems with companies that don't want to design sustainable gadgets, and how it all kind of sucks for the gorillas.

That's a lot of information to put on a poster. How are you going to do that? Psst— it doesn't matter if you aren't a dab hand at drawing. You can make it an informational poster, with only cleverly-placed text on it, or use stick figures to make your point. What's important is to get your message across.

TO DO OR NOT TO DO,
THAT'S REALLY UP TO YOU

ACTION 1
Cut the trash in your house by half

This one is easier said than done, and so it needs to start with a house meeting. Get everyone to study the house trash, give them T for Trash Troll and A for Agreeable Amigo and R for Rockstar Recycler when you grade their findings.

Here's the methodology (use big words to impress upon them the seriousness of this task).

The source of trash: First, identify where your trash is coming from—kitchen, bedroom, bathroom, study, and what kind is it. Categorise it into wet, dry, and other waste.

Audit the trash: Next, figure out what can be sent for recycling, what can be composted, what can be reused, what can be reduced. Like using two sides of paper instead of one and crumpling it and dunking it in the trash can. Or what can be cut out (see that's 4 Rs for you) like not buying bottled water. Refuse the Refuse (pun alert!).

Trash Tax: Enforce a trash tax. Anyone who gets a plastic bag from shopping instead of carrying their own pretty cloth bag has to pay Rs 10 to the Trash Tax Inspector (that's you!).

Change shopping habits: When going out for a walk or picnic or trek, carry a reusable water bottle from home. Not only do you save money, but also most mineral water bottles are made out of super cheap plastics and leach toxins after a period of time. And worst, the water often can be contaminated. Replace tissue papers with cloth napkins that can be washed, buy bigger size containers than several smaller ones.

See what can be reused: Get creative with leftovers—fried potato peels make amazing snacks and if not, can feed the compost. Yesterday's cauliflower veggie can become today's stuffed paratha.

See what can be upcycled: Ah come now, you have art class. Make lamps out of plastic water bottles and craft from wooden pencil shavings. You don't need anyone to tell you that.

Jot down your ideas for reusing and recycling here.

_____

_____

_____

_____

_____

_____

_____

_____

_____

_____

_____

_____

_____

_____

_____

_____

_____

_____

ACTION 2
Become a biographer of an object

Biographers are cool people, they may lead boring lives—of course, they don't *cough, cough*—but they get to write about interesting people.

Why don't you write about an interesting object?

Say, the journey of a pen from the time it was manufactured and then what happens when it's old and leaky and thrown out. Does it land in the landfill, does it get a swirl in the trash vortex or is it made out of recyclable material and becomes a clip then?

_____

_____

_____

_____

_____

_____

_____

_____

_____

_____

_____

_____

_____

_____

_____

_____

_____

_____

ACTION 3
What's the inside of a bin like?

EEEEEEEEEEEEEEEEEEEEEEEEEEEEEWWWWWWWWWWWWWWWWWW!
Imagine if you were a trash can, would you be down in the dumps
(note: pun 3)? Or would you be trash talking?

Think of what's it like to be a bin.

- How would you smell?
- What would you see?
- When different kinds of trash fall inside you, what sound do
  they make?
- How would it feel to touch a banana peel, a crumpled paper
  or tea leaves.

_____

_____

_____

_____

_____

_____

_____

_____

_____

_____

_____

*Note to parents: We did not ask your child to sit inside a bin. We asked them
to use their imagination. If they are sitting in a bin, that is not the publisher's
responsibility, or the author's!*

ACTION 4
Bottle up

You know how much a mineral water bottle sucks? Can you think of 15 ways to reuse a plastic water bottle? That's right, 15. It can be an art installation, a DIY craft idea, a... okay, now you think.

1. _____
2. _____
3. _____
4. _____
5. _____
6. _____
7. _____
8. _____
9. _____
10. _____
11. _____
12. _____
13. _____
14. _____
15. _____

Was that hard? Easier to use a refillable water bottle?

ACTION 5
How many parts?

This isn't an easy challenge.

You need to pick your favourite gadget.

Now that is easier than the next ask.

Find out all the materials that went into making the gadget. Doesn't matter if it's a tablet, a television, phone, X-Box or PS3.

Got the list?

There's more.

Find out if each of these parts are recyclable. Many groups in cities offer spaces where you can drop your old gadgets and they recycle them properly. Look them up.

_____

_____

_____

_____

_____

_____

_____

_____

_____

_____

_____

_____

_____

_____

_____

WATER

WHEN A LAKE BECOMES A WASHING MACHINE[1]

'Huh! Is that snow?' Neha was awestruck by the soft white flurries that swirled on top of Bellandur Lake in Bengaluru. The flurries looked strangely beautiful, like someone had let the washing machine run riot and now it was spewing froth and foam all across the lake. Or at least Neha thought it looked like that.

'Snow in Bengaluru? That's ridiculous,' said her friend Abhiyan, who had come over to play *MineCraft*.

As they looked at the lake full of froth, it started to rain. The froth spilled onto the roads, obstructing traffic. There was a disgusting stench around the lake, as if piles and piles of garbage was rotting away.

Neha and Abhiyan quickly closed the window. Off they went to the Internet to look up the news to figure out what exactly was happening.

'The stink is like a smelly armpit multiplied by 320 million litres,' said Neha.

'Why that much?' asked Abhiyan.

'Every day, Bengaluru spews out 1,100 million litres of sewage, but so far, the city can only treat 780 million litres. The rest gets dumped into lakes along with effluents. As a result, ammonia and phosphate levels go up and that's the froth right there.'

As they read on they found that the detergents used to wash clothes have a lot of phosphates and foaming agents

---

[1]http://www.bbc.com/news/world-asia-india-34376988

which also add to the froth. Neha and Abhiyan looked at each other and grinned. Their joke about the washing machine lake was true!

A few days later, Neha sent Abhiyan a photo message. The froth on the lake had caught fire! The chemicals in the foam had reacted and poof! up in flames the lake went. A burning lake, who would have thought?

What's in our detergent?

The dirty water from our washing machines is drained out into water bodies and pollutes them. A lot of detergents have phosphates to soften hard water and clean better. However, in many countries, phosphates are banned. That's because phosphates[1] cause eutrophication, a process which

---

[1]http://www.downtoEarth.org.in/interviews/detergents-threaten-indias-waterbodies-16470

increases micro-nutrients in a natural waterbody such as a river, stream or a pond. This increases the growth of algae and impacts the natural balance in the water body. When algae die and decompose, it removes the water's oxygen, which in turn affect the fish adversely. As the detergents destroy the surface water tension of the water, fish also end up absorbing more pesticides and pollutants in their body. People eat fish, as do other animals and birds. That means, we are also eating all that gunk!

But that's not all that pollutes water bodies.

WHAT'S UP WITH ALL THESE WATER BODIES, ANYWAY?

About 71 per cent of the Earth is covered with water, and many people think that because of this we will always have enough water. Yet a full-blown water crisis is a threat looming in the near future. Most of the water in the world is in our oceans, and is too salty for us. Scientists and engineers are figuring out how to desalinate water, or take the salt out of the ocean water. Only 2.5 per cent of that water is freshwater, the kind we can turn into safe drinking water. And only 1 per cent of that freshwater is water we have easy access to in rivers, aquifers, rain, etc. The rest is trapped in glaciers. At this point, don't be a wise girl or guy and say 'Hurrah for climate change that will melt the glaciers!' Seriously, don't even.

So even though most of our world has a LOT of water, we actually have very LITTLE water we can use and must use it wisely. Have you ever faced a morning where there was no water in your bathroom tap for a morning bath? Seen people queuing up by a community tap? Or water tanks coming to housing societies to provide water? Water scarcity is very much a problem.

India, for one, is a water-stressed region. Right now we have 1,122 cubic meter utilisable freshwater per year, per capita. But the international standard is 1,700 cubic meter, so we are way lower than that. The amount is supposed to go down to 1,000 cubic meter[1] in the future. That water is also not distributed equally—some people in our country have enough water to wash their cars and take long baths, while others have to walk for hours to be able to get a tumbler of drinking water.

It's really unfair—well-to-do people can install pumps, storage tanks and call for tankers when their water supply goes down. But people with less money can't do that.

India depends on its rivers and lakes for water. Yet, we are continuing to pollute them. Industrial effluents, domestic sewage, pesticide from agriculture, eroded soil, over withdrawal of water and religious practices are terrible for our water bodies. For instance, latrines and septic tanks pollute almost 80 per cent of surface waters in India[2]. EWW!

---

[1] base.d-p-p-h.info/es/fiches/dph/fiche-dph-7825.html

[2] http://www.waterworld.com/articles/wwi/print/volume-30/issue-2/technology-case-studies/urban-water-management-in-india.html

So then, what happens to a water body that has so much filth? Can it choke up and die?

Yes, it can. Ganga, along with Indus, Nile, and Yangtze is now classified as one of the ten most endangered rivers globally. And that's because of pollution, over-withdrawal of water and harsh climate conditions.

The Aral Sea[1], which was once Asia's largest lake, has now shrunk to one-tenth of its size from fifty years ago.

---

[1]news.nationalgeographic.com/news/2014/10/141001-aral-Sea-Shrinking-drought-water-environment

You are grounded! A.k.a. groundwater aquifers.

Your exciting Geography lessons must have told you by now that groundwater is water that's below the Earth's surface.

We don't see groundwater, because it's under the... yes, you're right, ground. But it is super important for all ecosystems.

When it comes to using groundwater, India tops the list globally[1]. Over 60 per cent of irrigation and 85 per cent drinking water come from groundwater. Yet, we are fast depleting our groundwater, which means that we could have a serious problem on our hands.

Then what will we drink? Colas? They need water to make too. In fact, soft drink companies have been accused of over-extracting groundwater for their factories and creating water shortage[2].

KINDA CURIOUS, HOW MUCH DO WE PAY FOR WATER?

No, no. Don't you go looking for a mineral water bottle to see the price of water. That is not what water costs. Did you know that you pay for the water that comes to your house? It takes a lot of work to get safe drinking water to people. If you are living in a city, then most probably the water has come from far—either from villages far away or sources that are deep in the ground.

---

[1] http://www.worldbank.org/en/news/feature/2012/03/06/india-groundwater-critical-diminishing

[2] http://www.righttowater.info/rights-in-practice/legal-approach-case-studies/case-against-coca-cola-kerala-state-india/

It takes massive amounts of energy to pump, treat, and deliver water to our homes. Then once waste water leaves our houses, we need energy to collect and treat that water before we discharge it into rivers. Energy to transport and treat water and waste water is expensive. In many cities around the world, the utilities that provide our drinking water and treat our waste water consume more energy than homes or businesses.

But the problem is we don't pay enough for these services. Some people believe that we pay almost 25 per cent lesser than what it costs to operate and maintain the systems that get the water to us. This is a major challenge because every human has a right to safe, clean, sufficient water. But it costs a lot of money to ensure that right.

And since we don't pay enough for water, it's hard to keep maintaining pipes. Which means leakages that leads to water shortage because of wastage. Makes you want to go and yell GAH!

Water rate

A water rate is charged for supplying water to either a public or private system to ensure sustainable water management and distribution. In cities, for instance, the water demand is around 135 litres per capita daily (lpcd) but in villages, it's 40 lpcd[1].

---

[1]http://www.livemint.com/Opinion/97fuaF2aQkO9IjPiPAjMyL/Six-charts-that-explain-Indias-water-crisis.html

The real price of bottled water

Bottled water is so horrible for the environment and often has contaminants. Crazy! But then sometimes you're travelling and you don't always get clean, safe water for consumption. Then the only option is to buy bottled water. When you do buy bottled water, make sure the plastic bottle gets recycled properly. Else, off it goes down our waterways, polluting our oceans and causing havoc for marine life.

HEY, CAN YOU HEAR THAT GURGLING SOUND? DOWN, DOWN, DOWN THE BIN. THAT'S WATER GOING DOWN THE BIN.

Suppose you have a leaky tap at home, and it leaks three litres per hour ever day (you can put a bucket and measure it. But no, instead go repair it. Stop procrastinating). How do you know how much water is being wasted?

Count the number of drips in a minute and then visit *http://water.usgs.gov/edu/activity-drip.html* to actually count the litres of water down the drain.

But apart from leaky taps, when you waste food, you're also wasting water.

Say you had an apple and roti sabzi in your dabba. You ate the roti sabzi, but didn't eat the apple. It lay forgotten in a corner of your bag, shrivelling up and becoming smelly, until your classmates complained, and you had to chuck that mega-old apple. Congratulations. You've just flushed 80 litres of water down the drain!

One apple that's chucked in the bin means you may as well be pouring 80 litres of water away. That's 80 medium-sized bottles down the drain.

Stop yanking my chain, you say? It's simple logic.

In order to grow food and even make clothes, agriculture needs water. That includes irrigation, processing, transport, the entire super-long process. To grow enough cotton for a pair of jeans[1], it takes something like 6,813 litres of water!

In India, we waste almost 40 per cent of the food produced, even before it gets to our homes[2]! That's a little less than half. In fact, we waste as much food as much is eaten in the whole of the United Kingdom.

How much water do we use across the world when it comes to food?

Something like 3.8 trillion m^3 (cubic metres) per year! Seventy per cent is used for agriculture[3]. According to a report, *Global Food: Waste Not, Want Not*:

Food for 1 person: 3,000 kcal per day by 2050

Diet: 80 per cent plant + 20 per cent animals

Water needed to produce that amount of food: 1,300 m^3 per person per year.

That's half an Olympic-sized swimming pool per person. If you haven't seen one, then look for one. These pools are huge!

---

[1]http://www.treehugger.com/clean-technology/how-many-gallons-of-water-does-it-take-to-make.html

[2]http://thecsrjournal.in/food-wastage-in-india-a-serious-concern/

[3]http://www.imeche.org/docs/default-source/reports/Global_Food_Report.pdf?sfvrsn=0

That's nuts!
It takes 4.16 litres of water to grow one almond[1]!

RACK YOUR BRAINS
Want to know your Water Footprint?
Then visit *http://waterfootprint.org/en/ resources/interactive-tools/personal-water-footprint-calculator/* to calculate how much water you use and waste.
Note it down here.

_____

_____

_____

THEY SAY THAT THE NEXT WARS WILL BE NOT OVER OIL OR LAND, BUT OVER WATER. IS THAT TRUE?

Out of the seven billion people on Earth, almost one billion

---

[1]http://www.motherjones.com/environment/2014/02/wheres-californias-water-going

don't have access to safe drinking water. That's one in seven people[1].

What is believed is that when two countries share water basins, one will use the other as 'leverage'. For example, although India and Bangladesh share fifty-four rivers[2] between them, there's always been some trouble about sharing it. Tsk tsk, don't they listen to moral science mottos? Love thy neighbour as you will unto yourself.

You can see the same thing happening between Karnataka and Tamil Nadu, over who gets what share of Cauvery's water.

In fact, some think that water use will become a weapon! Like closing access to water or contaminating it deliberately. That will be super nasty, and it's not the same thing as hosing someone down as a prank.

SO ARE WE DOOMED TO A THIRSTY FUTURE? WHAT NOW?

You know the answer. Come on now. It's simple—DON'T WASTE WATER.

These are simple tips:

▸ Turn off taps while brushing your teeth.
▸ Take shorter showers. Ooh maybe you can time your family.
▸ Fix leaks immediately.

---

[1] http://www.theguardian.com/environment/2014/feb/09/global-water-shortages-threat-terror-war

[2] https://globalvoices.org/2012/06/08/india-bangladesh-water-disputes-and-teesta-river-diplomacy/

▸ Water plants with (non-toxic) recycled water.
▸ Wash your bicycle with a bucket not a hose.
▸ Don't waste food and water.
▸ Eat local fruits and veggies because it takes a lot of water to get them to travel to you.

And it's easy enough to think of more ways. But the question is—will you?

Postcard from Katy Lackey
Big time savings for water

Katy loves chai but for that she needs water. Which is why she works as a research specialist at the Water Environment Research Foundation in Virginia. She also spent six years working with World Camp, Inc. in Lilongwe, Malawi, and in Ahmedabad to keep her tea supply going. Okay not really, but she did that mainly to improve community health while protecting natural resources.

Finding and fixing leaks in our water infrastructure is one of the most important things we can do to conserve water (and energy!). This is difficult because almost all of the pipes that carry our water through cities are buried in the ground and we don't see what happens to them. On average, cities around the world lose 30 per cent of the water in their system through leaky pipes. In many developing countries the loss is closer to 50 per cent.

This means that half of the water we take from rivers or pump from aquifers and treat for human consumption never actually reaches us! This is called non-revenue water because the utility pays to pump and treat it, but it never gets delivered to us, the consumer. Think how much water we could save, if all the water we take was used.

We can recycle plastics, glass, and many other things, but is it possible to recycle water?

Yes! In fact, in a sense, all water we use to drink, cook, wash, or make things is actually water that has been recycled many times already. It has changed form again and again, but the planet as a whole has not lost or gained any water. Scientists say that, technically, we are drinking the same water the dinosaurs did millions of years ago.

So all water is recycled over time. Nature slowly breaks down the contaminants that people, animals, and industry put in water by using it. As water flows in rivers, through soils into the ground, or evaporates back into the air only to come down again with the rain, it is cleaned and replenished.

But the cool thing is that we can speed up this natural process. There have been many advancements in technology that allow us to purify waste water coming out of our homes into water even cleaner than water in a protected river.

Waste water is the dirty water that flows from toilets either back into the river or to the treatment plant in our city or town. Many people are afraid to drink waste water that has been recycled, because it sounds gross to drink. Recycled water is a great way to conserve water, however, and as more and more areas face drought and water scarcity, we will have to get over this yuck factor. Remember, we are already drinking recycled water!

Just a few years ago, Witchita Falls in Texas had so little water due to a long drought, that the town began using recycled water for drinking. People learned how the water was purified and once they tasted it, they realized it was just like their other drinking water. In Singapore, people have been drinking recycled water for years!

But most places will have to pass specific laws and regulations before people can start drinking recycled water. For now, many water scarce areas around the world are already using recycled water for irrigation (agriculture takes a LOT of water). Hopefully recycled water for drinking will be next.

Postcard from Mithil Shah
Rain, rain, come again

Mithil has a boring (okay, not that boring) 9 to 5 job in Scotland but he has studied sustainability and lectures all his friends about rainwater harvesting. Like he's just about to lecture you.

Much of India depends on rain when it comes agriculture. But we need water for pretty much everything. Lakes and rivers are good examples of harvesting fresh water—they capture rainwater naturally. Rain water is also captured by the ground and that replenishes ground water levels.

Here's what it's like to do rainwater harvesting at home. Imagine this: When it rains, take one bucket or lots of buckets and fill them up with rainwater. When the buckets are full, quickly transfer the water to big tanks and fill them up. Similarly, rainwater harvesting system is like a big bucket that can be set up on a terrace or a garden to capture rainwater and safely save it in the tank or ground. If an entire community or building shares the cost of rainwater harvesting, then it's not expensive. If we don't capture rainwater in cities, it drains away, into the sewage and back into the sea.

How can one tank make a difference?
If everybody harvests fresh water, our water problem will reduce. Save every drop and it will create an ocean, similarly save every drop of water and we will need less fresh water from the lakes and rivers since we have our own source of water.

How is my local government helping me?
It is compulsory in most states across India to do rainwater harvesting[1], especially in new buildings. This includes Himachal Pradesh, Gujarat, and Tamil Nadu. In some of the metros, new buildings will not be given Occupational Certificate without rainwater harvesting systems.

WHAT DID PEOPLE IN ANCIENT INDIA DO WHEN THEY DIDN'T HAVE COOL TECHNOLOGY LIKE WE DO NOW?

Actually, they have done very well, some even better than us.

Ever seen a step well? It's a deep well with steps cut into its side so you can climb down to draw water. Called 'vav' in Gujarat (that is not wow in doge speak) and 'baolis' in Rajasthan, step wells have been used to store and manage water resources since the tenth century BCE. Step wells were used for irrigation—water was channelled to the fields. Most step wells were intricately carved and beautifully designed. In fact, they were also hang-out places for locals, because the water kept the place cool. See, that's why they didn't need air-conditioning back then. Also it wasn't invented yet, but that's beyond the point.

---

[1]http://www.rainwaterharvesting.org/policy/legislation.htm

Go tripping

Rani-ki-vav in Patan in Gujarat was built in the eleventh century CE with seven levels of staircases. Intricately carved, the well was designed as an inverted temple, because water was considered sacred.

RACK YOUR BRAINS

Research online or in books for indigenous ways of storing and managing water in India. Step well is one example. Many communities in India have their own ways of conserving water. Here are a few names of practices to get you started. See if you can match them to the part of India they come from.

▶ Johads
▶ Check dams
▶ Vav
▶ Naulas
▶ Dongs
▶ Bamboo drip irrigation
▶ Ahar pynes
▶ Dungs
▶ Bhandaras
▶ Virdas
▶ Pats (not the one you give on backs)
▶ Keres
▶ Zings

Meet India's Water Man

Who needs Iron Man and Spider-Man, when there's India's Water Man. Rajendra Singh has been working in the arid landscape of Rajasthan with communities to revitalise precious water resources. Using traditional practices of rainwater harvesting, Rajendra Singh worked with the community to repair, maintain and build traditional check dams or johads, so that villagers can conserve rainwater, instead of relying on bore-wells that deplete ground water. In 2001, he received the Ramon Magsaysay Award for Community Leadership.

Also, meet Aabid Surti

Aabid Surti is a writer and painter who lives in Mumbai. He's also someone who cannot stand to see water wasted. But unlike most people he didn't just repair his tap leak and was contented. Instead, he started the Drop Dead Foundation.

As his website, *www.ddfmumbai.com* reveals:

'In 2007, Aabid launched Drop Dead Foundation after a leaking faucet at a friend's house bothered him so much and caused an epiphany. Since then, Aabid's Drop Dead team (consisting of a plumber, a volunteer, and Aabid himself) makes the rounds every Sunday fixing plumbing leaks in the Mira Road suburb where he lives. Today, Drop Dead Foundation continues to provide free plumbing services to Mumbai households.'

Aabid Surti is eighty-one years old and making a difference, one leaky tap at a time.

SO MANY MEN,
WHERE ARE THE WOMEN IN WATER?

In rural parts of India, women are responsible for managing water for the household. In fact, every second woman there has walked some 173 kilometres to lug water in 2012. That's because they don't get water piped into the house. Instead, they have to walk for kilometres and kilometres to fetch water. Some even walk up to 10 kilometres and others have to go six times to fetch water. These are not paved roads we are talking about. Also, a filled up pot is as heavy as your school bag would be if you put all your books inside it. Walking long distances to collect water in many parts of the world can be dangerous for young women (or men).

India   Africa   Latin America

There can be all sorts of violence they are subject to. Often girls miss out on school because they have to help out at home in tasks such as these.

RACK YOUR BRAINS
As cities go deeper and deeper into villages to meet their water requirements, will women have to walk longer distances? Can you think how not having water for sanitation impacts the health of women and children and the environment? When there's less water, how does it affect nutrition for children and families?

TO DO OR NOT TO DO, THAT'S REALLY UP TO YOU

ACTION 1
Make it rain

With temperatures rising and plummeting, rainfall patterns are getting disrupted! Here's a simple experiment where you can create your own rainfall, inside a glass jar.

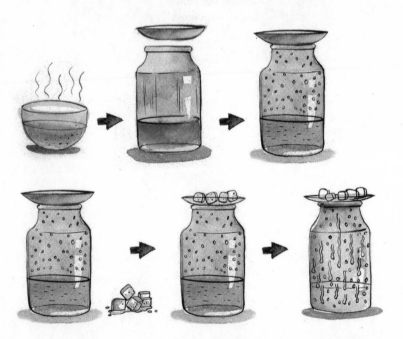

Fill a bowl with hot water. Now pour it into a big glass jar—about one third—and cover it with a glass plate. Condensation will start forming on the sides.

While the jar sits on the table, get some ice cubes from the fridge. After a minute put the ice cubes on top of the plate. You may not hear thunder, but it will begin to rain inside the jar. Water droplets will form and trickle over the sides of the jar.

Now you know what Zeus or Indra feels like.

The science is simple—there's warm air inside the jar. The ice makes the plate cold, and the warm air rises up, condenses, and forms water droplets.

Too easy?

ACTION 2
Create a rain cloud

Let's take it up a notch, and make a rain cloud!

You will need a glass jar, shaving cream, water mixed with food colour.

Fill the jar three-fourths with water. Now spray a generous amount of shaving cream on top and cover the surface of the water. That's your cloud.

Drop the coloured water and the food colouring slowly on top of the shaving cream. You can use a pipette. As the shaving cream cloud gets full of water, it will start falling through the cloud, to the ground. That's just like clouds that fill up with condensation, gain mass and then it rains.

You will see swirls of clouds forming in the water below the shaving cream.

ACTION 3
Conduct a Water Behaviour Audit

A Water Audit does sound Very Important, and it is. And honestly, we just cannot trust the adults alone with something as precious as water.

Audit your family members by asking them about their attitude towards water—you can add your own questions if you like. Recommendation: Wear a lab coat, carry a clipboard, and make Hmmm sounds to each response. Works without the props as well.

Here's the scoring sheet:

Never: 0

Sometimes: 5

Always: 10

Questions

1. I shower for five minutes and not more...
2. When brushing my teeth, I turn off the water................................
3. I use the garden hose, instead of a bucket and mop, while washing the car/scooter/bike ....
4. I repair leaking tap immediately...
5. I run the washing machine when it's full..
6. I call the plumber when the toilet starts leaking............................
7. Our building does rainwater harvesting..
8. Our building recycles grey water..
9. I reuse water from the kitchen and bath for watering plants.......
10. Make your own question...

Now tally up the answers and make some deductions. A lot of water waste is about our behaviour and attitudes. If we think it's okay to keep the tap running while brushing teeth or ignore a leaky tap, we are part of the problem.

ACTION 4
Calculate your food's Water Footprint

Here's a guide to calculating the water footprint of your food.

Typical values for the volume of water required to produce common foodstuffs:

Foodstuff	Quantity	Water consumption
Fruits and veggies		
Apple	1 kg	822 litres
Banana	1 kg	790 litres
Tomato	1 kg	214 litres
Cabbage	1 kg	237 litres
Olives	1 kg	3,025 litres
Potatoes	1 kg	287 litres
Meat		
Beef	1 kg	15,415 litres
Chicken	1 kg	4,325 litres
Pork	1 kg	5,988 litres
Sheep	1 kg	10,412 litres
Carbs		
Bread	1 kg	1,608 litres
Pasta (dry)	1 kg	1,849 litres
Rice	1 kg	2,497 litres
Dairy		
Butter	1 kg	5,553 litres
Cheese	1 kg	3,178 litres
Chocolate	1 kg	17,196 litres

Milk	1 × 250ml glass	255 litres

Others

Pizza	1 unit	1,239 litres
Tea	1 × 250 ml cup	27 litres
Egg	1	196 litres

Source: **Global Food: Waste Not, Want Not** *by Institute of Mechanical Engineers*

Calculate how much water would it take to make:

Pasta with olives and tomatoes

_____

_____

Omelette with cheese and tomato

_____

_____

A meal with chapati and potato veggie

_____

_____

A meal with rice and sheep meat

_____

_____

Your favourite meal

_____

_____

ACTION 5
Become an oil spill offender

What's an oil spill? Not the one when you're cleaning your bike and spill oil on your nicest pair of shorts. Anyway, who told you to wear them while cleaning your bike? Don't listen to those detergent ads on telly. An oil spill also isn't the one where you squirt cooking oil across the stove instead of the pan.

If you tried cleaning up the mess, then you know that water and oil don't mix. So imagine a shipload of oil falling into an ocean.

Yes, the ocean is vast but the damage that the oil does is HUGE. Especially to marine life and birds. It's really awful.

On 9 December 2014, an oil tanker had an accident and spilled some 3,50,000 litres of heavy fuel oil into the Shela River in the Sundarbans in Bangladesh[1]. Sundarbans is known for its tigers, dolphins, and mangroves and is a UNESCO World Heritage and Ramsar site.

Wonder how do you react to that? 'Uh, Oh, Sorry!' doesn't quite make it okay.

Alright. Now it's time to simulate an oil spill in your home[2]. Here's what you need to do.

Fresh water

Fill a glass bowl almost to the brim with cold water. Add a few drops of food colouring and mix.

---

[1]http://www.eecentre.org/ReportDetails.aspx/id/51/lan/en-US
[2]Source: Minister of Supply & Services Canada, 1994

Crude oil

Take a mug and mix 3 tbsp vegetable oil with 2 tbsp cocoa powder.

Now slowly contaminate the fresh water by pouring in the 'crude' oil. What happened? Does the oil float above the water? Record your observations.

Next, dip a bird feather into the oily water. What happened to the feather?

The impact of an oil spill is horrendous for the ecosystem[1].

- The oil slicks over birds' feathers and they can't fly. They eventually die from the cold. Any oil on their eggs will also harm the chick inside.
- Oil also damages the internal organs of birds.
- Otters need clean fur to stay warm. But when oil coats their fur, they become cold and fall ill.
- It also impacts snails, clams and other life that live on beaches.
- Even small amounts of oil can cause major problems in baby fish.

---

[1] http://response.restoration.noaa.gov/oil-and-chemical-spills/oil-spills/how-oil-harms-animals-and-plants-marine-environments.html

WILDLIFE

WHEN TWITTER IS DOWN

Suhani woke up one day to no twittering. She couldn't understand where her sparrow and parakeet pals had gone. She had gone to her grandparent's place for the summer holidays and got back late last night. Usually she woke up to the birds' tweets and chirps, along with her mother's rousing yell. But today it was only her mum going, 'Suhani, wake up.'

She rubbed her eyes, 'I am awake, Mum,' she said. 'Calm down now.' Suhani clambered on to her window sill and looked out.

'Mum!' Suhani said frantically. 'It's gone. Our jamun tree. They cut it down.'

Suhani's mother came running into the room and joined her by the window sill. 'Oh no,' she said softly, caressing Suhani's hair. 'I am so sorry, darling. I fought the committee against the decision to cut down the tree, but Rai Uncle insisted that the tree's branches were creating problems in our neighbours' houses.'

'How can trees cause problems?' Suhani bit her lips and tried not to cry looking at the sorry state of the tree. It had been hacked—its branches sawed away, all its shiny, green leaves carted off to some other location, and no more promise of fat, purple jamuns. And its citizens—the birds— had left the tree in search of a new home.

Suhani was going to miss the sparrows and rose-ringed parakeets. And the butterflies and insects.

Suhani's bird friends left because their tree home was cut down. But sparrows and bees are also disappearing. Any clue why?

Plants need pollinators such as bees, butterflies, beetles, bats, and hummingbirds for fertilization and reproduction. However, the indiscriminate use of pesticides is killing bees and other pollinators. That's because pesticides don't know the difference between good and bad pests always—so for them an evil weevil and awful aphid is the same as a busy bee and a beautiful beetle.

The other problem is that as we have more and more concrete around us, and less green spaces. This habitat destruction is threatening bees. But without pollinators, there's not much scope for food for us.

These are pretty much the same reasons you're seeing fewer house sparrows around. In fact, scientists also say that electromagnetic pollution from mobile phone towers is affecting sparrows' reproduction.

But I do see more crows, and kites around

Yes, as our garbage increases, so do the scavengers. Crows and kites are pretty effective scavengers—they feed on dead animals and plants as well as our garbage now. What they do is pick through our trash that's overflowing everywhere for tasty morsels for themselves. And which is why they are thriving.

THAT'S NOT ALL. SOMETIMES EVEN THE MOST INNOCUOUS LOOKING THINGS CAN THREATEN A FOREST.

Lantanas are those tiny flowers that grow wild on roads— white, pink, orange, yellow, in colours. You must have seen them while on a hike? Lantanas are pretty and they attract butterflies, but they are also weeds. Because lantana adapts and spreads easily, a lot of trees are being replaced by lantanas, which makes them an invasive species. Today they can be found on 13 million hectares land in India[1]! Researchers estimate that this invasive species made its way to the country sometime in the 1800s.

Animals that depend on those trees for food find that a problem. The lantana is a bush like shrub and has thorns and makes it difficult for animals to pass through.

Imagine a plant that was brought for the garden has now become a threat to our plants and animals! Who knew such a small action would have such big effects?

According to the UN Convention on Biological Diversity[2] alien plants and animals constitute 'one of the greatest threats to biodiversity, and to the ecological and economic well-being of society and the planet.' And already because of climate change, 20 to 30 per cent of plant and animal species are at an increased risk of extinction.

---

[1]http://conservationindia.org/articles/lantana-in-india-a-losing-battle/
[2]https://www.cbd.int/doc/publications/cbd-ts-01.pdf

SORRY TO INTERRUPT, BUT I HAD TO ASK—CAN TREES MOVE? (AND WE DO NOT MEAN THOSE FICTIONAL TREE ENTS FROM J.R. TOLKEIN'S *LORD OF THE RINGS*.)

Here's a real-life story that will give you a clue.

Karthikeyan S. is the chief naturalist at Jungle Lodges and Resorts. He loves trees. Once when he was taking a walk down Cubbon Park in Bengaluru, he stopped to pick up a core of the mahogany seed. The core was brown and looked like flat wings. The seed were neatly arranged around the woody core. Karthikeyan took a seed and flung it in the air, where it whirled like the blades of a helicopter. 'That's seed dispersal,' he said. 'And people say trees don't move. Then what is this?'

When you go on a walk, look out for fallen seed pods. They come in different sizes and shape. Some rattle, others swirl in the air, and some are thick and clumpy.

RACK YOUR BRAINS

How do trees communicate? Can they smell? Can they count? In fact, they grow in such a way that they don't block each other's sunlight. Now that's Tree BFFs. Actually, it's called Canopy Shyness.

So, how do you think trees talk to the birds and other animals that drop by to say hello? Do some research, find out how intelligent are trees.

Check out the book *The Hidden Life of Trees: What They Feel, How They Communicate – Discoveries from a Social World* by Peter Wohlleben.

Or simply, go and observe just one tree for at least a few weeks.

WHAT'S THE BEST WAY TO CONSERVE AND SAVE ALL THESE AWESOME TREES, ANIMALS, AND FORESTS?

Leave them alone! Nature doesn't need our help. Rather, we are dependent on Nature for everything—air, water, food, the works. Nature can survive without us, but we can't.

Our forests are falling to poorly-planned development—highways are being built through jungles and trees being cut down to make way for more agriculture or industries or houses. We need to stop using so much and taking so much from the forests.

Not only that, animals are poached for their skin, their teeth, their claws for really silly human greed. That horrible trade needs to be stopped by the stringent protection of forests and empowering forest guards to be able to combat poachers. We can do our bit by not buying anything made from wildlife—such as shell paper weights, peacock feather fans, and ivory bookmarks.

ANCIENT MAN AND ANIMAL DEPICTIONS

In the late 1950's something strange and wonderful happened. Dr Vishnu Wakankar, who was an archaeologist at the Vikram University in Ujjain, stumbled upon a set of prehistoric rock shelters outside Bhopal. The rock caves of Bhimbetka in Madhya Pradesh has paintings from the Lower Palaeolithic Age to the Early Medieval Ages. That's rock art which is 15,000 years old and can still be seen!

What's wonderful about the paintings are that the people back then used natural colours—red, ochre, and white—from leaves, flowers and so on. The scenes depict everyday life—dancing, hunting, riding horses and elephants, collecting honey, and lots of animals. There are elephants, tiger, leopards, bison, boar, deer, and peacocks painted across the rock shelters.

It shows how our ancestors had a complex relationship with animals. They were hunters and food-gatherers, and depended on the animals for food.

Look closely at these paintings, go on, pretend to be an art critic. And you will realize that there's a certain sense of awe for these animals and how majestic and beautiful they are. For instance, the Boar Rock is one of the most famous ones—it shows a giant boar, complete with troll-sized horns and whiskers chasing a human who is running frantically. Animals were clearly a big part of our ancestors' lives, whether it was for food, storytelling, art, and companionship.

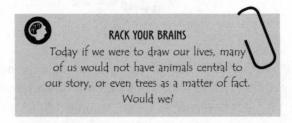

RACK YOUR BRAINS
Today if we were to draw our lives, many of us would not have animals central to our story, or even trees as a matter of fact. Would we?

THE TIGER-FOREST-WATER CONNECT

There's a saying that Bittu Sahgal, the wonderful editor of

Sanctuary Asia, often tells children. He says:

'If you save the tiger

You save the forest

You save our precious water resources'

How you ask?

The tiger sits at the top of the food chain. That means tigers are also indicators of a healthy forest and that there is the correct balance of prey and predator.

Forests are home to over 600 rivers and streams that provide drinking water for us. Moreover, forests are carbon sinks—they take carbon dioxide from the atmosphere. When it rains, the jungle acts like a sponge, taking in the water, retaining it in the soil, making it rich and fertile. And of course, storing water.

For Bittu Sahgal, the Maths is simple:

Tigers = Forests = Water.

Postcard from Prerna Bindra
The bear necessities

On most days, Prerna would prefer to be in the forest. But because she has to write about them and fight to protect them, she often ends up being chained to her desk. An author and wildlife conservationist and a fierce protector of wildlife, Prerna explains why meeting a bear in the wild is special.

I wander around a lot of forests, and people always ask me: Aren't you afraid, being in forests among wild animals? No, never. Unlike what most people think, wild animals are not ferocious, out to kill you, or attack you. They will only strike back in self-defence, if we attack them, or if they feel cornered or frightened, or when defending their babies. I have walked in forests for years, and met elephants and bears, and lions and leopards. But, look, I am alive to tell the tale! Like the time when I met a Mama Bear and her cub. We were walking in the Dachigam forest in Kashmir. I was with a forest guard, a small-statured, brave man who had walked in these lovely forests for many years. We had gone inside the park for some work, and decided to trek back. It was getting dark.

As we turned a corner, we almost stumbled onto a Himalayan black bear, taking the same turn from the other side! We were shocked and so was the bear! She was carrying her young one on her back—bears carry their cubs like that. The guard pushed me to the back. And the Mama Bear? She quickly set her cub down, tucking it inside the bushes by the side of the path, and then turned around to face us. She stood on her hind legs and lifted her front legs...it was a pose that made her seem bigger, brawnier and scarier. We stepped back, slowly.

Having given a warning not to mess with her, she quickly gathered her cub and vanished into the jungle.

And we sighed in relief.

The encounter taught me many lessons that day. We must always be careful in the forest, and never be out after full daylight, when animals are most active. It disturbs them, and can lead to bad accidents. Talk loudly and make noise when you walk, so as not to surprise and alarm wild animals, who may panic and attack.

I learnt that animals warn you, give you a chance...if you read their language.

Most of all, Mama Bear taught me that animals love their children too, that their first instinct is to protect them from any danger—just like our parents do.

HOW LOVELY. MEETING A BEAR! IT REMINDS ME OF AN ELEPHANT I SAW IN A CIRCUS. HE WAS PLAYING CRICKET. IT WAS GREAT FUN.

Not for the elephant, it wasn't. Wild animals don't belong in circuses or entertainment zones.

If you've been to a circus, then you may have seen elephants standing on two legs, bears riding a cycle, and tigers jumping through hoops of fire. They don't do this in the wild. This isn't natural behaviour for them. (Don't give silly arguments like there are no cycles in the wild.)

Instead, they are trained to perform these silly tricks through starvation and cruelty. Thankfully, now wild animals are not allowed to perform in circuses in India. There's a law against it.

For those of you who have been to places like Sea World, it's lovely to see a dolphin or a seal up close. But they belong in the oceans and rivers. Imagine having an entire ocean to swim in and then suddenly being made to balance a ball on your snout in a tiny swimming pool. It's like being confined in a room for the rest of your life. And they didn't even do anything naughty for being grounded.

These animals live in groups and living solitary lives in

a tank isn't fun for them.

What you can do is not visit so-called entertainment places. If you want to meet animals, then observe them in their natural habitat.

OKAY OKAY, BUT WHAT IF WE CAN'T GO TO A FOREST? THEN WHAT?

To see animals, birds and plants, you don't always have to head to a forest. (Though it would be nice to be able to do that.) There is plenty of wildlife around you in cities.

Lizards on your wall that call tock, tock, tock
Woodpeckers on trees that go knock, knock, knock
Owls in the trees who hoot, hoot, hoot. Though it
sounds more like a hiss, hiss, hiss.
Bats that make high-pitched sounds and fly over your
head. No, they don't want to get entangled in your
hair. That's a myth, please.
Birds, oh so many kinds of birds, rose-ringed parakeets
and peacocks, and sparrows that know how to keep
their cool when it's hot.
Butterflies flitting about in cities. If you're in Mumbai
look for the Atlas, the world's largest moth.
Even snakes are sometimes curled up in a tree hole,
mind you.
Slender loris on tree tops are quite a few,
Flamingos visiting city swamps,
Vultures roosting in old monuments and having a
romp.
How did you miss all of those now?
How, how, how?
All you need is a keen eye, no don't frown,
And a dash of curiosity, to make some wild friends
around town.

RACK YOUR BRAINS
Make a better poem about the urban
wildlife in your city.

Flamingos you say?

Every year, Mumbai's skyline becomes tinged with pink as tens of thousands of flamingos visit the Sewri Mudflats between November to March. This otherwise marshy and polluted industrial area suddenly looks like someone has blown pieces of cotton candy on it, letting it settle down and giving the landscape a vibrant hue.

The term flamingo is said to have come from flamma, the Latin word for flame, leading to its other name—the firebird. Apart from the flamingos and the extremely noisy seagulls, people can spot the Indian pond heron, egret, ibis, black-tailed godwit as well as various species of eagles.

Most people puzzle over the fact that there are two kinds of flamingos at the bay. While some are pink, the others are grayish white. The reason? Flamingos are born gray-white and turn pink after two years. Their plumage turns pink due to a carotenoids-rich diet—blue-green and red algae, insects, crustaceans, mollusks, and small fishes. In fact, birds in captivity have been known to turn pale, unless their diet is supplemented.

Inspired by the flamingos, photographer Ashima Narain directed *In the Pink*, the first-ever 'urban wildlife' documentary to focus on this avian phenomenon in Mumbai. Ashima was fascinated by the fact that flamingos were thriving in the midst of a populated metropolis. 'Here in Mumbai's own backyard, you have these birds. It's a fantastic urban phenomenon,' said Ashima. 'It's strange—on one hand, you have this breath-taking sea of pink, yet they are set against a backdrop of a power plant, a ship-breaking yard, petrochemical industries and a fertiliser factory. It's quite a spectacle.'

THE ATTACK OF THE NINJA CROW

Taranjit Chhabra had a strange problem. Whenever she would go outside her house, a crow would come swooping down, cawing loudly and would try to peck her with a very sharp beak on the top of her head. And a crow's beak is quite sharp, in fact, it's called 'the Swiss Army knife of beaks'[1] because it can slice, cut and rip through a lot of things. So imagine a Swiss Army pecking away at your head! OUCH!

It became so bad, that Taranjeet couldn't go out of her house without ducking and sprinting to her car. Finally, the family decided they needed to decipher the Attack of

---

[1]https://books.google.co.in/books?id=FrG8pIQ5WJkC&pg=PT59&lpg=PT59&dq=swiss+army+knife+crow&source=bl&ots=_0gIa5tgaQ&sig=hW3mm2eF76MEE9Jjghop8G_QnHM&hl=en&sa=X&ved=0ahUKEwidmdewwabJAhWBBY4KHc3gDEwQ6AEIKTAD#v=onepage&q=swiss%20army%20knife%20crow&f=false

the Ninja Crow. After careful observations, they deduced that the Ninja Crow was a Mommy Crow. Her nest was in their garden, right above the place where Taranjeet burnt some garden leaves. Garbage smoking is also injurious to the babies' health. No wonder Mommy Crow became a Ninja Crow.

After that, Taranjeet stopped burning the leaves there, and Mommy Crow left her alone.

So what does that prove? Should we all wear helmets to protect ourselves from the Attack of the Ninja Crow?

It shows that animals are smart, even though human beings think they are smarter. Crows are part of the *Corvidae* family, and have large heads. They are intelligent birds with powerful memory skills. In fact, one study[1] said that they may have the reasoning ability similar to a seven-year-old child. The study which observed New Caledonian crows in New Zealand said that the crows are the only non-primate species that can make tools. These birds fashion hooks to pick out grubs from logs.

Not surprising that this particular Mommy-Ninja Crow did not forgive Taranjit. Doesn't it make you wonder that we are surrounded by all sorts of animals, birds, and insects. But we don't realize how our small actions may have a huge impact on them.

---

[1]http://www.dailymail.co.uk/sciencetech/article-2590046/Crows-intelligent-CHILDREN-Study-reveals-birds-intelligence-seven-year-old.html

Then why is anyone stupid called bird brain? Think I am one, huh?

Just because birds have small heads, doesn't mean they are stupid. In fact, a German[1] study showed that captive European magpies, *Pica pica*, can actually recognize themselves in the mirror as well. That's called self-awareness, something scientists until now only believed was shown by chimps, dolphins, elephants, and, of course, us.

The next time you call someone chicken, remember this study from researchers at the University of California[2], San Diego School of Medicine which revealed that chickens had a comparable neocortex physical structure—the part of the brain that handles complex cognitive (of the mind) functions. Now that's something to cluck about, for chickens at least.

Birds, for instance, can do things that we can't. Unlike us, owls don't have symmetrical ears. That way owls can get to their prey quietly and swiftly in the darkest of nights.

As silly as a superstition

Did you know, in some cultures owls are considered inauspicious. So when they come and perch on a tree, happily snoozing away after a night jaunt of rat hunting, people throw stones at them to shoo them away.

---

[1]http://scienceblogs.com/grrlscientist/2008/08/19/magpies-challenge-bird-brain-m/

[2]http://ucsdnews.ucsd.edu/archive/newsrel/health/07-02avianbrain.asp

RACK YOUR BRAINS

It makes you think that if birds are like us—or are we like them—then what about other animals? How similar are we, say, to a rat, a dog, or an octopus? Or what makes us different?

◇ Elephants travel in packs, they are super intelligent, they mourn for their dead, and take care of their young ones.

◇ Birds know how to navigate and travel long distances, something we can't do without Google Maps now.

◇ Like no two people have the same finger print, no two tigers have the same stripes.

◇ Leaf-cutter ants are also farmers with underground fungus farms.

Do some research and record your observations and findings.

In some cultures, a black cat crossing the path is considered bad luck. 'Why did the black cat cross the road?' 'Because it wanted to spook humans out.' Sounds like a silly joke doesn't it? How can someone crossing a road be bad luck for anyone? Unless they don't look left and right before crossing.

Animals are often worshipped—such as elephants and snakes, but at the same time they are mistreated horribly.

I once knew a rat snake (he was non-venomous, most snakes are not poisonous) who had become blind because humans kept worshipping him and applying red tikka powder on his forehead which harmed his eyesight. When I rescued him from a snake charmer, he was blind as a bat.

And had diarrhoea from being starved and then force fed milk, which For Your Information, snakes do not drink. That is a myth. Nor can they can hear very well, so if you've ever seen a 'snake dance' they are only following the movement of the been, the musical instrument.

P.S.: If you see a wild animal in distress, don't handle it yourself. Instead call your local Society for the Prevention of Cruelty to Animals or Wildlife Authorities.

THAT'S TERRIBLE. I DO LOVE ANIMALS AND WOULDN'T TREAT THEM BADLY. I HAVE A PAIR OF BUDGIES IN A CAGE.

So, breaking news: Birds don't like being in cages. Here's one such real-life bird story[1].

Shawnu was a rose-ringed parakeet—he sat dolefully on a window ledge. Like countless other birds raised in captivity, Shawnu couldn't fly because his wing feathers had been clipped. All he could do was hop from one place to another. He sat on the wrong side of the window—inside a house, rather than outside perched on a tree or flying happily with his friends.

Rescued from a fortune teller by volunteers of the People for the Ethical Treatment of Animals (PETA) in Mumbai, the rose-ringed parakeet was tiny, almost as if his growth had been stunted from spending a lifetime in a dingy cage the size of an iPad Mini. When anyone came close to Shawnu, he would fluff up his feathers, roll his eyes in fear and make an angry, throaty sound. He constantly groomed himself,

---

[1] A version of this story first appeared in www.dailyo.in

to the point that his fragile body was dappled with bald, grey patches. This obsessive, repetitive behaviour called zoochosis is often seen in animals in captivity.

Who could blame Shawnu for being so angry and frightened of human beings? Although trade in indigenous (local to our country) bird species is banned in India, thousands of parakeets, munias and other birds are snatched from their forest homes and smuggled in atrocious conditions to different parts of the country and the world, destined to live a miserable life in captivity. They are stuffed down water bottles, put inside socks and transported from one country to another.

Three cheers for the law

In 2015, the Delhi High Court recognized that 'Birds have the fundamental right to "live with dignity" and fly in the sky without being kept in cages or subjected to cruelty' and 'running their trade was a violation of their rights'. India has strong laws to protect wildlife. The Wildlife (Protection) Act, 1972 prohibits the trade in over 1,800 species of wild animals, plants and their derivatives, and so does the Prevention of Cruelty to Animals Act, 1960.

But ultimately, this violation of rights is down to our apathy and greed. Our desire for trapping these winged beauties has led to centuries of torture and violence on birds.

There's nothing more wonderful than watching a bird in the wild—whether it's a pair of brown sparrows scratching in the dust, a serpent eagle perched majestically on a tree or an owl peeking out of her tree hole. And you don't have to visit a forest to watch birds.

On hot summer days, leave out a bowl of fresh water for birds on your window ledge, and parakeets, mynahs and sparrows will swing by for a drink or two. Or look out of your balcony to watch kites soar gracefully above the cityscape. Free like that, it's not hard to understand, why the caged birds do not sing.

Companion animals

Do you know PETA doesn't use the word pets? It prefers the word Companion Animals, because aren't they just that?

Remember, getting an animal home is a responsibility. You have to feed, bathe, clean their poop, take them for walks. Dogs and cats don't mind being with humans. But snakes, turtles, fish, birds belong in the wild.

If you're considering getting a ~~pet~~ companion animal, then adopt them, don't buy. Contact your city shelter to adopt a puppy or a kitten who needs a home. After all, animals aren't 333333333commodities.

Postcard from Reena Puri
Johnny, Johnny

When Reena is not taking care of her many dogs and cats, she is also the editor of Amar Chitra Katha. As a member of Save Our Stray NGO in Mumbai, Reena remembers a dog who couldn't walk at all.

Johnny, a street dog, was in a bad shape. The vehicle that had struck him down had crushed his lower back and his spine had been damaged. He could not move at all.

And then it poured buckets and buckets on 26 July 2005 in Mumbai. The poor dog was stuck with nowhere to go and the water level was rising. One kind person lifted him up and put him on higher ground under a shop's awning.

The Save Our Strays ambulance parked outside our friend Namrata's house became Johnny's home. We made him as comfortable as possible on a pile of sheets and newspapers. A timetable was drawn up and a few of us volunteers from SOS, living nearby, were given time slots to clean, feed and medicate Johnny every day. He needed someone to do that thrice a day. He needed to be turned as well so that he would not develop bed sores.

Johnny got used to our coming to take care of him and always rewarded us with a wag of his tail and a lick. He was in terrible pain but would only cry out a bit when we turned his side. He never lost heart while he was with us. He would lie quietly, his beautiful young face watching the door till one of us arrived. He loved the food we brought him and lapped up every bit of it.

A month passed and then another two weeks. The monsoon arrived and the ambulance could no longer be parked in the open. Animal shelters were full. We moved the ambulance to my parking lot in the society where I stayed. After cleaning and sponging him and when there was hot food in his belly I would often just sit and talk to him. None of us ever got tired of looking after Johnny. We wanted to see him walk.

Despite all our efforts Johnny developed a nasty bed sore which only grew in size. We needed to clean and dress it every day.

Finally, we got a message that we could admit Johnny to the Welfare of Stray Dogs in Mahalakshmi. There he was given more medical help and physiotherapy. When we went to visit him he would brighten up and want to come back with us. Johnny died, leaving us feeling empty and bereft. He was very special. He brought so many of us together. He actually cemented the foundation of SOS. He loved each one of us and taught us to spread that love to many more animals.

TO DO OR NOT TO DO, IT'S REALLY UP TO YOU

ACTION 1
Let the wild rumpus begin

If you don't know what book that quote is from then, ten points from Whatever House You Are In. (Answer: It's from Maurice Sendak's *Where the Wild Things Are*).

Grab a notebook and pen or pencil, or if you have to, the doodle pad on your tablet. Draw yourself, your family, and friends. Stick figures are totally allowed.

Now draw the environment around you. Where you live, school, park (if you have one), mall, and so on. Squiggles with labels will also do.

Next, draw animals, forests, water bodies.

Sign the drawing. Ok not really.

Some questions for you:

- How far are the animals from you? What kind of animals did you draw?
- How far is the park as compared to your school for you?
- Is the forest close by?
- Why did we draw this differently from our ancestors? When did we become the sort of people who don't like nature around us?

ACTION 2
Become a Nature Detective

It doesn't matter what your window looks out to. Even if you can barely see more than that grouchy uncle who lives in the opposite house, find a place where you can see some trees. It is not that hard.

What you really need is a keen eye and a curious nature. Something like the Famous Five and David Attenborough.

You don't need a magnifying glass though it helps when looking for insects. But you do need a notebook to record your observations, a flora and fauna book for identification, pen or pencil, and a bag to store all of these in. You can get some excellent material from the Bombay Natural History Society. Look them up online.

Now step out and look outside.

LOOK PROPERLY. Stop getting distracted by the TV or tablet. Oh sorry, you can look at the book. That's totally allowed.

What do you see outside your window/ balcony/ garden/peep hole?

Stay still and be quiet, very important skills for an observant detective. For those who are living in concrete jungles called cities it doesn't mean that flora and fauna aren't around you. Look closely at a gulmohur tree—you will see rose-ringed parakeets lounging on its spindly branches, creating quite a racket in the mornings and evenings. Or crows and kites that are everywhere, flying from one building to another, or circling lazily for prey in the morning sun. And what about that brown sparrow making circles with its tiny body in the dust? The sparrow, in case you were wondering, is taking a dust bath which helps maintain its feathers.

Ants, creepy crawlies, dogs, cats, animals, birds, and insects are all around us.

ACTION 3
Seasonal help

If you're feeling the hardships of the weather, imagine how animals and birds feel? They don't have fans to keep them cool, heaters to keep them warm, and water filters to give them fresh water in the summer.

As the seasons change, step into an animal's furry paws, and try and think what they need. Here's a suggested list:

Summer

It gets really hot in most parts of India, and while we can escape it by swimming or sitting under a fan, animals can't do that.

Birds don't sweat and their body temperatures are much higher than other animals, but they have built-in systems to help them beat the heat. This includes breathing faster, bigger beaks, and bare skin patches that allow heat loss.

But when the temperatures are soaring, they feel the heat as much.

Make sure you leave out a bowl of water on your window sill or garden for thirsty birds. Set up a bird house to give them some respite from the sun.

Keep a bowl of water out for cats, dogs and larger animals as well.

Monsoon

When it rains, animals often get stranded. Look out for hurt or injured animals and call a local NGO to come and help.

Insects often get trapped in puddles, and you can lift them gently with the help of a dry leaf and put them back on a plant.

ACTION 4
Hold a wildlife film screening

Gather some friends or family and watch a wildlife film. This can be any of the following, these are just suggestions:

- The BBC series *Planet Earth* presented by David Attenborough: A look into some of the wildest, most beautiful parts of our planet.
- BBC's *Natural World Special: Queen of Tigers:* The story of Ranthambore Tiger Reserve's Machli, one of the most famous tigers in the world.
- Ashima Narain's *In the Pink:* The film looks at the phenomena of some 20,000 flamingos coming to Mumbai every year.
- The Bedi Brothers' *Cherub of the Mist:* A film about red pandas in the wild. There are barely 1,000 of these elusive animals in the world. The filmmakers go to Singalila National Park in the Eastern Himalayas to find these endangered animals.

See what's available in your local library or iTunes, Netflix, YouTube etc.

Watch a film with your friends and discuss the movie. Put on your film reviewer hat and say what made you like the movie (or not like it), did it make you want to visit the forest or ocean where it was shot, and what message did the film have.

ACTION 5
Collect and create wild words

What are wild words?

In his book *Landmarks*, Robert MacFarlane collects words associated with landscapes. He calls them 'place-words'. For instance, *quealed* is a word for vegetation that has withered and curled up. In Cornwall, *zawn* is a word for a 'vertical fissure or cave cut by wave action into a coastal cliff'.

How visual are these words? Can't you see grass that's all quealed up under the searing heat? Or a round indentation in a mountain created by water that looks like a deep zawn.

When you go out into nature, can you come up with your own lexicon? Or pester adults to tell you old, forgotten words for nature.

For instance, *aandhi* is such an appropriate word for a sandstorm, because it blinds you as well. Then there's *cloud bobs*, a word a friend invented for fat clouds on a sunny day. They do look like blobs of cotton, don't they?

So it's your turn now, collect leaves, gather memories, assimilate words associated with nature. And where you can't find an appropriate word, conjure them up.

THE END

OKAY, NOT QUITE, A SMALL LECTURE IS DUE HERE

Congratulations!

You've finished reading this book. Or well, you skipped a bunch of chapters, and landed up right here, at the very end. Either ways, you're kind of an Ecovestigator, Greenetective, Enviroagent, Conservationsleuth. Well done.

This is to certify that

_____

has read this book.
signed:
The Earth

But before you frame that certificate, a few more things.

We live in an imbalanced world

One thing's kind of clear—everything is inter-connected. Climate change, water, food, waste and its impact on human beans (As Roald Dahl's Big Friendly Giant would call us) and flora and fauna and vice versa!

These impacts, however, aren't felt equally by people across the globe. For example, the weather gets hotter, some of us can afford to switch on our air-conditioner and close the door on the world outside. Yet, millions of people including children can't do that. Some don't even have homes, let alone fans and ACs. When it gets cold, it's not pleasant being out on the streets, or in a home without a heater. People die from intense heat or cold waves.

We already know that with unpredictable weather, food prices will be affected. Some of us, again, will be able to get food from across the world, where there may be more optimum climate conditions. But not everyone can afford expensive food. Food is a basic human right, and by making it unaffordable, we are violating that right when someone goes to sleep hungry.

The same goes for water—as cities go deeper into villages for precious water, the people who live there get affected. They have to walk for hours to get water, stand in line, and sometimes do without water. And that's because a handful of people waste more water or pollute it, making it undrinkable for others. When conditions become harsh, families are often forced to migrate. They come to the cities and find daily labour and their quality of life is not very nice.

This unfair distribution is a form of social and environmental injustice. A lot of the issues that you read about in this book affect poor children more than upper middle class and rich children.

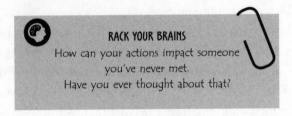

RACK YOUR BRAINS
How can your actions impact someone you've never met.
Have you ever thought about that?

SO, WHAT NOW?

Can you figure out the one thing that connects the points below?

▶ Our climate
▶ Our water
▶ Our air
▶ Our natural world of animals and plants
▶ Our food
▶ Our people

That's right! The word 'Our'. We are part of the environment and dependent on it. Yet we are destroying it at the same time. So strange!

Of course the grown-ups are wrapped up in some strange environment versus economic debate. Some of them think that for India to develop economically, we need to dam water, cut down forests and mine hills. But let's face it, development means having clean air, fresh water, and lots of green spaces. So then there's really no debate, is there? We're all on the same side—development that's green, good for the economy, and that benefits *all* people, and not just a few rich people.

P.S: Check out the book, So You Want to Know About Economics *by Roopa Pai, to understand some of the gobbledygook behind economics.*

THEN, IT'S UP TO THE YOUNG GENERATION TO PROTECT THE EARTH! GO TEAM YOUNG ONES!

Annoying isn't it when adults tell you that? The grown-ups are supposed to be the responsible ones, the ones who have figured it all out. But there we go, chasing fossil fuels, wasting food, destroying our soil with pesticides, filling up landfills, and cutting down forests.

Most of us don't do that directly. We don't take a saw to a tree and cut it down. It's pretty hard to do that, just to let you know.

But our actions are responsible for that. So while we may be part of the problem, we are also part of the solution. What say?

Recycling, consuming less, buying from farmers, aiding conservation measures, supporting green policies by voting for politicians for whom environment is important (well, when you are eighteen of course), our collective actions are important.

Enough of the doom and gloom. Look around you. We are such an integral part of that awesome thing called nature.

There are mighty trees that line our roads, some there

for years and years, even before our grandparents. An entire
ecosystem of birds, flowers, insects, fruits live in those trees.
For those of you lucky to live close to the sea (or well, now
with climate change, perhaps less lucky), there's the constant
ebb and flow of the tide, the little crabs that scuttle around
in the waves, the shells that insects leave behind. Others
have an unparalleled view of cloud bobs around them, the
mountains wrapped in clouds and snow, or forests that are
home to water and wildlife.

It's hard to imagine our Earth without all of this.

There are small things we can all do:

▶ Spend a little time outdoors—take a walk, look at the
  mysteries of nature, why are the ants so busy, why do
  leaves turn red, or just enjoy the walk. And feel, what
  Rachel Carson, calls a sense of wonder. (It's also healthy,
  by the way).
▶ Become a biophile, and not biophobic. Biophilia is love
  for nature while biophobia is a fear of it.
▶ Save, don't waste.
▶ Conserve and protect what you love—chocolate,
  animals, water.
▶ Spread the word.
▶ Add your own thoughts here.

ACKNOWLEDGEMENTS

Writing this book was as challenging as finishing my Math homework while I was in school. Mainly because, as a grown-up, I managed to find more important things to do such as baking cookies or doodling, instead of writing. But now that the book is done, it's down to the people on this page.

My mother, Jayshree, was the one who showed me what it means to have love and concern for all the wild things and their forests. My father, Mayur, encouraged me and made sure I had all the books I needed, even if he wouldn't get me a dog. My sister, Chaitali, who gave me my first wonky fringe, has been unwavering in her support, as has her husband, Salil. Thank you Narendra Kaka and Yamini Kaki for being amazing.

The idea of this book took form at Sangam House, the wonderful residency organised by Arshia Sattar, D.W. Gibson and Rahul Soni in Nrityagram. Thank you Sreelata Menon for the fellowship. Am ever grateful to Stephy, Suhani, Shinibali, Lalitha, Mithil, Namrata, Deborah, Neha, Hashim, Amit, LOW Lives, as well as Chitra, Fiona, Amrita, Jairaj, Rohini, Dharini, Ruth and Abhilasha.

I am fortunate to have had wonderful mentors including Bittu and Madhu Sahgal, Ingrid Newkirk, Jason Baker, Will Bates, Naresh Fernandes, and Nandini Ramnath. A place that's special to me is the University for Peace in Costa Rica, where I studied climate change. Thank you Greg, Katy, Suroor, Jen, ESP, CPC, and my professors Jan, Stephen, Rolan, Eric, Rob, and Reg. This one's for Mahmoud.

Sayan, whose illustrations give meaning to this book, it was fun working with you. And Mohit for this gorgeous cover. The wonderful team at Red Turtle, including Mugdha and Shreya. Rrishi Raote for proofing the book with an eagle eye. A big hug to Vaishnavi, Tsitsi, Tendai, Maegan, Raju, and Mathangi who read my manuscript and to Roopa Pai and Jerry Pinto who gave me confidence. A warm hug for my friends and contributors Prerna, Dilpreet, Nirmal, Kartick, Zack, and Ashima.

There are some people without whom this book wouldn't be complete. Sudeshna, my publisher and friend, for her unwavering faith, warmth, and timely stern emojis. Deepanjana and Gauri, for love, laughter, tissues, and a pair of very able shoulders each. To J.K. Rowling who doesn't know me, but continues to inspire me with her magic tapestry of words. And Abhiyan who makes me believe in the beautiful things in the world. He also eats all the cake I bake while procrastinating.